Execution, Plain and Simple

Execution, Plain and Simple

Twelve Steps to Achieving Any Goal on Time and on Budget

ROBERT A. NEIMAN

McGraw-Hill

New York   Chicago   San Francisco   Lisbon   London
Madrid   Mexico City   Milan   New Delhi   San Juan
Seoul   Singapore   Sydney   Toronto

The McGraw·Hill Companies

1 2 3 4 5 6 7 8 9 0   DOC/DOC   0 1 0 9 8 7 6 5 4

ISBN 0-07-143888-2

This publication is designed to provide accurate and authoritative information in regard to the subject matter covered. It is sold with the understanding that neither the author nor the publisher is engaged in rendering legal, accounting, or other professional service. If legal advice or other expert assistance is required, the services of a competent professional person should be sought.

—From a Declaration of Principles jointly adopted by a Committee of the American Bar Association and a Committee of Publishers

McGraw-Hill books are available at special quantity discounts to use as premiums and sales promotions, or for use in corporate training programs. For more information, please write to the Director of Special Sales, McGraw-Hill Professional, Two Penn Plaza, New York, NY 10121-2298. Or contact your local bookstore.

 This book is printed on recycled, acid-free paper containing a minimum of 50% recycled, de-inked fiber.

Contents

Contents

ACKNOWLEDGMENTS

"People read about execution, but say, 'I still don't know how to execute. What do I do first, second, third, etc.?' Can you answer that question?" asked my publisher. I started to spin out my answers and after many weeks of debate, we had what turned out to be the table of contents of this book. I then drew on my recollections and experiences to set down the ideas, stories, and tools that have ended up on these pages. In the process I drew on many other people directly and indirectly.

Robert H. Schaffer, founder of our firm, gets major credit for key concepts. Ron Ashkenas, currently one of our managing partners, got me into the publishing mode, and saw to it that I had the time and support needed. Robert and Ron both read and commented on the early drafts.

Members of the firm of Robert H. Schaffer & Associates provided input in review meetings and individually: Katy Bevan, Suzanne Francis, Claude Guay, Rick Heinick, Elaine Mandrish, Nadim Matta, Matthew McCreight, Keith Michaelson, Patrice Murphy, Katy Paul-Choudhury, Rudi Siddik,

Acknowledgments

Wes Siegal, Harvey Thomson, Justin Wasserman. Dick Bobbe, retired partner, contributed basic disciplines of the practice. Emilieanne Koehnlein prepared the text for submission. Amy Beebe and Maura Pratt provided administrative and marketing support.

Richard Narramore was the McGraw Hill editor. Hilary Powers, copy editor, made the original text more readable.

Managers in companies such as Allied Signal, AMAX, CNA, GE, Hartford Financial, Motorola, *New York Times*, PNC, Provident Mutual Insurance and others, and public service enterprises, such as the New York State Education Department, Memorial Sloane Kettering Cancer Center, Philadelphia Department of Human Services and others, were actors in cases in this book. John Murphy, head of Executive Edge and an articulate spokesman for "Results First Development," and Chris Trani, a talented internal consultant, provided practical suggestions.

Supportive family members provided perspective. So thanks to Debbie, Susan, Peter, and Megan.

Robert A. Neiman
Robert H. Schaffer & Associates
30 Oak Street
Stamford, Connecticut 06905
e-mail: ran@rhsa.com
Phone: 203/322-1604
Web: www.rhsa.com

Introduction

Better execution is one of the great untapped opportunities for improving organizational performance. Yes, it is basic. Yes, it is what managers do all the time. Yet, in too many organizations, execution falls inexcusably short.

Moreover, despite its importance, execution has been in the background of management thinking, taken for granted, dismissed as obvious, even considered mundane in contrast with the sparkle of new strategies, new technologies, new opportunities, and new partners. Execution as a competitive advantage has been hidden behind a thick curtain.

My colleagues and I have been working with leadership organizations for more than 40 years to help accelerate achievement of goals and build execution capability—with continuing success. But the subject of execution has never been popular.

Until recently.

In their book *Execution: The Discipline of Getting Things Done* (Crown Business, 2002), Larry Bossidy and Ram Charan raise the curtain.

Introduction

They direct a spotlight on "execution cultures" where *exemplary* on-time, on-budget, on-spec performance is a vital key to exceptional results. Jim Collins in his book *Good to Great* brings into the focus the power of steady, step-by-step, accelerating growth of performance—execution—holding to sound, basic strategies. Nitin Norhia in his research of more than 160 companies during 10 years found execution along with strategy as a prime determinant of organizational success. These findings and publications have brought execution front and center.

These books and much of the literature of management and change tend to focus on the job of the CEO and senior managers charged with governing and leading the total enterprise. *Execution, Plain and Simple*—the book you are holding now—places the spotlight on all those other people who must lead execution: the team leaders, supervisors, unit managers, plant mangers, sales managers, division heads, and business unit heads and others as well as chiefs who have to deliver results. Whereas most books focus on "the architecture of execution," this book concentrates on frontline implementation. It presents ideas, tools, and cases to demonstrate effective execution in practice. It is designed as a field guide to help managers tackle opportunities they are working on now, and also to serve as a guide for the development of up-and-coming managers.

Structure of the Book

Part I outlines 12 basic steps to accomplishing any goal on time and on budget. These 12 steps represent basic disciplines—the things that need to be done in the process of executing an assignment or an opportunity.

Part II then addresses "accelerated execution" and what my colleagues and I call *"zest,"* the fuel for getting people to use the 12 steps and build higher performance and greater execution capability in the organization. The zest factors help harness the electricity of crisislike events, but in small-scale, rapid-cycle, breakthrough projects. In such projects managers step up to higher goals and learn to use execution disciplines to escape the embedded organizational, psychological, and cultural barriers that put a false ceiling on organizational performance.

Introduction

Parts I and II fit together and reinforce each other. By doing better at executing goals on the one hand and tackling tougher and more far-reaching goals on the other, managers build an ongoing process for growing achievement and increasing capability. In this way, execution becomes a virtually no-cost path to higher performance, greater productivity, more successful innovation, and more rapid change. You won't need new facilities, new tools, complex systems, or heavy-duty training programs to realize this added boost to performance. You can start small—with changes in the next 30, 60, or 100 days—and see dramatic payoffs with resources available right now. And the payoffs multiply as the organization expands its execution capability. This makes the application and practice of the disciplines of execution (often seen as dull, niggling detail) exciting and worthwhile.

You might well ask why execution is so important.

First, there is enormous untapped potential in organizations. Look past the gleaming apparent performance of almost any organization and you'll see flaws of execution under the surface—work started but not completed, work delivering less than promised, time and budget commitments not met, errors and rework from mere trivialities to huge and costly oversights. In addition, tensions, conflicts, neurotic behavior, and turf and political battles drain energy and impede progress toward worthwhile goals. Harnessing just some of that lost energy produces a huge boost in performance.

Second, change has reached a new order of magnitude in today's tumultuous markets, with their digitization, high-speed communications and global reach. Too many organizations are disappointing their constituents and even failing outright. Managers find it easy to rationalize these failures by pointing to factors outside themselves, but the truth might well be that they simply need to execute far better to keep up with and get ahead of the rapid change that confronts them.

Third, managers can learn many subjects in formal schooling, in on-the-job training, and in management development exercises. But where do they learn execution? How do they learn to push through the realities of strategic dilemmas, resistant organizations, political undertow, and bureaucratic mazes to pull together all the elements needed to get results? Managers have to learn these realities of execution on their own. They have to relearn these realities in every new organization they work with and on every new project they tackle. But learning from experience based on the systematic thought and discipline outlined in this book builds sustainable capability, which cannot be acquired any other way.

The Source of the Insights

This book is based on direct experience. My colleagues and I have been working with managers at all levels in many industries around the world. We have learned to make development of execution capability and culture a concrete, predictable process. Using the ideas presented in this book, work groups have increased their productivity by 30 percent and more in weeks. Big losses have turned into sustainable profits in months. Product development cycles have shrunk from years to weeks within a few months of beginning the effort. Information system installation times have been cut in half and payoffs have grown. Accidents and injuries have decreased dramatically within a matter of weeks. Agricultural production has increased threefold in months. Stable businesses have grown. Dispirited cultures have come to life. Rigid, self-involved cultures have opened up and sought change. In these and many more cases, the main thing that changed was the level of execution.

The bottom line:

- Managers can improve performance and achieve substantially better results by focusing on execution improvement.
- Execution capability improves when managers focus on urgent goals and use small, short-term "breakthrough projects" as real-life laboratories for building the skills, processes, and tools of execution. (The message of Part II.)
- The gains begin immediately. The returns can be astounding, and they can be multiplied with repeated success.

This book offers a framework for execution discipline. When you read it and use it, you will be able to execute your immediate goals, build longer-term execution capability, and focus your organization on the major strategic objectives it must achieve.

Execution, Plain and Simple

PART I

Twelve Steps to Achieving Any Goal on Time and on Budget

Part I examines each of 12 basic steps of execution in some depth. You might ask, "Do I have to do all this to execute successfully? It seems like a lot of work."

Well, it's like learning any disciplined activity—sports, musical instruments, or new software. It might seem awkward and slow at first. With practice and successful experience, you move faster, you become more versatile and find creative ways to use the basic steps effectively as you need them. Good execution becomes natural and effective when it is based on very solid grounding in all the basic disciplines.

In the increasingly networked, integrated, worldwide environment of management, many of the old structures, ground rules, and practices of bureaucracy fade away. Managers must become much more adept at these basic disciplines of execution, which still stand as pillars of successful management.

Design for Success

1

Take Responsibility–
Who, Me?

The underlying assumption of execution is that your own sense of
responsibility and your initiative will be the driving forces for achieving
your goals. All the tools and techniques work only in the hands of a responsible initiator.

Taking responsibility and initiative has several meanings.

If you are managing an effort, it means you have the responsibility for
its success. You look ahead, anticipate what can happen, and take action
before the fact to deal with it.

If you are party to an effort and see an error being made or an opportunity to do something better, you raise the issue and do something constructive about it.

Taking responsibility and initiative is not a problem for entrepreneurs
or solo operators whose whole work existence depends on their own initiative. Taking responsibility and initiative is not a problem for managers
in complex organizations who have a clear assignment, enthusiasm about

tackling the assignment, plenty of people and resources available to help, and who feel confident they can carry it off.

As a leader, however, you will encounter frustrations.

You may not see a direct connection between yourself and the issue to be addressed. You might ask "Why me?" Or say, "I'm not ready, someone else is more qualified." Or, "I don't know how to deal with this."

Delays, unexpected changes, off-target work by subordinates or team members, squirrelly activity by other departments, and just plain mistakes are all inevitable and will cause frustration.

Sometimes you'd like to say, "I can't accept the poor performance. So and so will have to be disciplined or transferred or fired." Or "It's up to the boss. He has to make clear what he wants to do." Or "Other executives have to make decisions and not keep backing down." Or "My people just have to realize they must take more responsibility." Or "If Marketing doesn't stop cutting prices, there is no way this business can survive."

True as these kinds of statements might be, and tempting as it is to shift the onus to someone or something else when things get frustrating, the hard fact is that when the time comes to really confront these issues and make something happen, you need to roll back the tape and ask what *you* might have done or not done that caused or exacerbated the problem. You'll need to ask yourself, What could I have done differently? Then you have to ask yourself, Given where we are, what should I do now?

If you are responsible, you'll take responsibility and initiative, not wait, deflect, or sidestep the issue.

This does not imply that you must feel impelled to act on every need and opportunity you see.

- Managers take responsibility and initiative when they see an opportunity they believe they can deal with successfully.
- Managers take the responsibility and initiative when they must do so because the issue is within their formal responsibility.

- Managers take responsibility and initiative when they see actions or inactions of others that might impinge on their sphere of responsibility.

Taking responsibility and initiative means that when you come to an impasse, a plateau, or a dilemma, you recognize that it is up to you to get the ball rolling.

The first step for execution is therefore mental preparedness. Think of yourself as someone who has an assignment or an opportunity and it's time to get moving. Think of the role you'll play. If you are a senior manager, you will be conceiving major directions and calling upon others to create work programs and specific projects. You will be acting as a sponsor. If you are a middle manager, you might be creating the work programs and projects. You might be a sponsor of an array of projects, or acting as a leader of a project, or you might be team-leading several projects. If you are a front-line manager, or are leading a specific project yourself, you'll be a project leader. If you are a staff person or facilitator, you'll be providing support. If you are a participant, you'll be carrying out specific tasks.

The basic 12 points of execution apply to any goal. Only the content and specifics change as you work down from broad strategic matters to very specific action projects. But it is important to be clear about the role you play so that you execute appropriately in your role.

This book is a job-aid or map of the territory to be crossed in executing any goal. It is written specifically for the primary leader—the one who has the main responsibility for accomplishment of a goal. It will also be useful for those playing other roles—sponsor, support person/facilitator, or participant—because everyone needs to understand and apply the basics.

To get maximum value, select something you need to accomplish now as a case to work on as you read through the material. Having a real project in mind will help bring the points to life. You might also come out with a better plan to tackle your project or carry out your assignment.

You can use the following worksheet to select your case.

WORKSHEET

Select a Case to Work On

1. What project or management challenge is at the top of your priority list now?

   _____

   _____

   _____

2. What do you need to accomplish? What is the *end result goal* you are shooting for?

   _____

   _____

   _____

3. What are the tough issues involved?

   _____

   _____

   _____

   _____

   _____

4. Who are the people involved?

   _____

   _____

   _____

5. What would you like to do better as you move ahead?

   _____

   _____

   _____

   _____

Take Responsibility—Who, Me?

6. What role will you be playing—sponsor, project leader, participant, or support person?

_____

_____

_____

_____

_____

_____

_____

_____

_____

_____

_____

2

What's That Again? Define Your Assignment–In Writing

Ideally, execution begins with an assignment—an official charge to tackle a goal. A good assignment generates a spark, enthusiasm, a spring to your step. It comes from your boss, your management team, or your board, and it spells out what you need to accomplish and gives you some guidance on how to proceed.

Ideally, you'd be able to discuss the assignment first, then you'd get a written memorandum summarizing it. The tone would be encouraging. You and your boss would both have a warm feeling that you are all together and off to a good start.

That would be ideal.

All of this might sound like the most basic aspects of Management 101. But because it is so basic, giving assignments is often slighted, treated inadequately or superficially.

You might discover that there are quite different views of just what the assignment really is. It might be ambiguous or confusing because it overlooks important questions, or has the wrong tone, or covers up hidden but important concerns. It's tempting to shrug and move on, doing the best you can. For effective execution, however, you must sort out the issues and define the assignment early on. Skip over this step, or leave it too loose, and your whole effort is on shaky ground.

While you might receive flawed assignments, certainly you don't want to convey inadequate assignment to your own subordinates. So let's review the basic elements of assignment making.

A Good Assignment

An assignment has two dimensions. One involves the explicit expectations, and the other the hidden or implied expectations. It's essential to deal with both.

Explicit Issues

- *Goal:* What is the end result to be accomplished and how is success to be measured?
- *Background:* What led up to the assignment and why is it being undertaken now?
- *Assignees:* Who are the people expected to complete the assignment, and with what authority and resources?
- *Timetable:* What are the dates for accomplishment of key milestones and the final results?
- *Reporting process:* To whom must progress be reported? How? When?
- *Structure:* How is the assignee to relate to other people and to other key parts of the organization?
- *Competing and supporting work:* How does the assignment relate to other initiatives going forward in the organization?
- *Guidance:* What are the policy guidelines and boundaries that govern the effort?
- *Consequences:* What are the rewards and penalties associated with the job?

Implicit Issues

- *Role:* How is the assignee really expected to act: As leader? Decision maker? Coordinator? Facilitator? Adviser? Political peacemaker? Diverter? Surrogate? Scapegoat?
- *Accountability:* Does the assignee have *prime* responsibility for accomplishing the results, or are other managers and other functions to share this responsibility? If so, how?
- *Capacity:* Are the assignee's skills, behavior patterns, and managerial adroitness adequate for the task, or is help to be provided? Is the assignee to be surrounded by people who can make up for gaps?
- *Tone:* Is the assignment a cloak for criticism of past work? Is it a test of capability to take on new responsibilities?

Note that an implication of criticism creates defensiveness just when positive attitudes are needed most. Criticism needs to be dealt with separately.

Make Sure the Assignment Is Solid

Once you have an assignment, the next step is to be sure it is clear and valid, and that you and other key people are on the same wavelength. There are several different ways you can do this:

- Talk with your boss and with others relevant to the assignment to test your understanding of and assumptions about the assignment.
- Draft your own view of the assignment, if a written version is not available, and talk it through with your boss and other key people.
- Sketch a preliminary plan to respond to the assignment, as a memo to discuss with your boss and others, and to test mutual understanding.

Taking some time to clarify the assignment is important. Sometimes just a little discussion will help a great deal. Sometimes more extensive work is needed. Here is one example where the surfacing of hidden assumptions underlying an assignment was very productive.

Dave, vice president of a mutual insurance company, was named project manager for a major new product. He was a long-tenured and highly respected manager who would be able to mobilize the rank and file of the traditional insurance operating organization. At the same time, he was able to work effectively with several new executives who were taking the company in new directions with powerful but highly complex new products.

Dave should have been pleased with his new assignment and the visibility it would provide. But he was concerned that the assignment just was not workable. In addition, another long-service executive who had been put in charge of a new corporate project had recently been let go when the project failed. Dave consulted his lawyer in case the assignment was a veiled matter of "age discrimination" that threatened to turn him out. He also insisted that there be discussions with the new executives, the president, and even the chairman to clarify the expectations and decide if the assignment were really feasible.

The discussions brought out many issues that hadn't been considered adequately before. The group dealt with questions about the roles and relative responsibilities of each of the other executives who would be part of the leadership team for the effort. It faced up to issues about the resources that would be available and issues about the priority the project would have in the Information Systems Development Group—which would have a very large job to do but already had a full workload. The assignment that finally emerged was a more thoughtful and thorough description of the project, how it would be led and managed, Dave's specific responsibilities, the roles of other key managers involved, and how the risks and rewards would be dealt with. And the possibility of being set up for failure was put to rest.

Take Time to Prepare Good Assignments

Both parties—the assigner and the assignee—share responsibility for the quality of an assignment. The assignment is a joint commitment. Each can take initiative to work toward clearer, more realistic and thorough assignments.

It doesn't take much time, often, to make a better assignment. Sometimes a few minutes of thoughtful dialogue can make a huge difference. The main thing is to define the assignment clearly and be sure all parties understand it.

Ray, head of a Commercial Insurance IT group, initiated a major improvement in his IT division. He started by formally assigning (with the aid of a 20-person man-

What's that Again? Define Your Assignment—In Writing

agement and planning team) three systems maintenance teams to generate a 25-percent increase in their measured productivity in three months. This was thought to be an unrealistic goal, given the oppressive workloads facing the whole IT function. However, it turned out to be just the stroke of lightning that reenergized the group. Two pilot groups achieved the 25-percent gain in less than three months, one going further and reaching 40 percent. New ways of setting priorities, new ways to combine work orders from client groups, more thorough work planning, regular measurement and feedback of actual performance—and just the charge to "do it"—accounted for the gains. As the productivity effort expanded to the entire department, a 26–work-year backlog was carved down to size, and the group shifted to a major new automation initiative to support a thorough redesign of the business while continuing maintenance support, without adding any people. Here's the assignment as Ray presented it:

From: Ray

To: [The three team leaders, by name]

Subject: IT Maintenance Productivity

This memo is to summarize our recent management team discussions about the need to increase productivity substantially for systems maintenance, and your assignment in particular.

We are facing a monumental challenge. Not only is there a huge backlog of work on our plates, but we are also expected to take on a major new automation initiative for the business in a few months. There is no way we can meet these challenges by just working harder and faster. We need to invent much better ways to carry out our work and introduce innovations to do what's needed at affordable cost.

To get started, the management team and I are calling on you to take the lead in demonstrating ways to do this. Specifically, we are looking to you to produce a 25% increase in maintenance productivity in your work groups in the next three months. This means getting 25% more maintenance work-orders completed each week with the same group of people you now have. It means continuing to meet customer requirements and maintain customer satisfaction. It means doing the work without short cuts that will cause difficulty later on.

We believe this can be done. There may be better ways to work with customers to define project requirements. Work orders may be grouped differently for more expeditious handling. Repetitive problems may be attacked with more fundamental improvement rather than repeated fixes. There may be better ways to handle the work within your groups. We don't know the answers. But we do have confidence that you and your team can come up with new ideas, better ways to do things and can demonstrate real success.

To get started, meet with your team to discuss this assignment. Outline your preliminary thoughts on how to proceed and a work plan for getting started. Show how you'll measure your productivity and track results. I would like to see your plan and review it with you in two weeks. Please set up a date on my calendar.

You can call on help from our consultants, other staff in the company, myself and other members of the management team.

This is a very important undertaking for our department and for the company. The management team and I look forward to working and learning with you on this effort.

The *key point* here is that before you get going on your effort, shape your assignment. Here is a worksheet you can use for the purpose:

WORKSHEET

Defining Your Assignment

Write an assignment for a current or proposed initiative—such as the one you've chosen for use throughout the 12-step process in this book. Cover the explicit issues:

- *Who is the initiator?* _____.

- *Who is the recipient?* _____.

- *Goal:* What is the end result goal to be accomplished? How is success to be measured?

  _____

  _____

  _____

- *Background:* What led up to the assignment? Why is it being undertaken now?

  _____

  _____

  _____

What's that Again? Define Your Assignment–In Writing

- *Assignees, Authority, Resources:* Who is to complete the assignment? What authority and resources will be available?

  _____

  _____

  _____

- *Timetable:* When are major milestones to be completed and the final results achieved?

  _____

  _____

  _____

- *Reporting process:* How is progress to be reported? To whom? When?

  _____

  _____

  _____

  _____

- *Structure:* How will the assignees relate to other people and to other key parts of the organization?

  _____

  _____

  _____

- *Competing and supporting work:* How does this assignment relate to other initiatives going forward in the organization?

  _____

  _____

  _____

  _____

  _____

- *Guidance:* What areas and issues are to be addressed? What are the policy guidelines and boundaries to be observed?

  _____

  _____

  _____

- *Consequences:* What rewards and penalties are associated with the job?

  _____

  _____

  _____

Implicit issues:

- *Role:* How is the assignee really expected to act on this project?

  _____

  _____

  _____

- *Accountability:* Does the assignee have *prime* responsibility for accomplishing the results? Or are other managers and other functions to share this responsibility? If so, how?

  _____

  _____

  _____

- *Capacity:* Are the assignee's skills, behavior patterns, and managerial adroitness adequate for the task, or is help to be provided? Is the assignee to be surrounded by people who can make up for gaps?

  _____

  _____

  _____

  _____

What's that Again? Define Your Assignment–In Writing

- *Tone:* Does the formal assignment suggest strong confidence in the receiver? Is it a statement of the importance of the job to be done? Is it a test of the assignee's potential for greater responsibility?

  _____

  _____

  _____

  What steps will you take to clarify or strengthen the assignment? With whom? When?

  _____

  _____

  _____

  _____

  _____

  _____

3

Organize Your Core Team and Create a Strategy

The previous chapter dealt with creating good assignments. Now we'll look at how you respond to them. Once you have a clear assignment, the next step is to form a core team and create a strategy.

Gathering a Team

It pays to assemble a core team, even though it might seem a burden at first. The payoffs come soon enough. You'll have a better plan. You'll have a corps of people to help manage the undertaking and to take responsibility for various parts of the effort. You'll have a consistent leadership group to see the project through to successful conclusion. You'll spend less time and energy running around chasing down every detail for yourself when the project moves into action.

Having several people involved, you and your team have another advantage. Team members will have several different points of view on how to approach the job, and very likely some ideas you hadn't thought of. Intensive and thorough-going dialogue will be needed to ferret out good ideas, generate consensus, and create the strategy. Normally this produces better strategy than one person's view alone.

Be selective when you make your choices for team members. The core team is the small group of people with whom you work most closely to plan and carry out the effort. Pick core team members for the following qualities:

- *Competence:* They each know something about the job to be done and can possibly lead a part of the effort.
- *Representative:* They are part of and can speak for specific constituencies.
- *Influence:* They can gain access and have a credible impact on some part of the organization or its stakeholder group.
- *Availability:* They can have time and energy to dedicate to the effort.
- *Loyalty:* They are aligned with you and have a sense of responsibility to work with you.
- *Candor:* They are open and willing to share their views. More important, you trust them and are willing to listen to them when they have criticism or views different from your own.

Building a Strategy

The strategy is the basic approach you will take to carry out the effort and will be the basis for detailed planning and action. The strategy need not be a firm plan at this stage. It's generally enough to tell the story of what is to be done and provide a flexible framework for further work. Flexibility is important in situations that are changing fast, and innovation and improvisation are crucial to success because there are many unknowns. This is true, for example, in product development for rapidly changing technologies or markets. Strategy can get into greater detail and be firmer early on in situations where the work is more familiar and more structured. This is true for basic manufacturing, transaction processing, sales, and construction work. Strategy sessions can get into considerable detail when all the key players are together and can dedicate sufficient time to details.

Organize Your Core Team and Create a Strategy

You and the team spell out the following factors:

- The goal to be achieved, measurements, and target date for getting the end result.
- The paths to be pursued to reach the goal.
- The people to be involved.
- Relevant data to establish the case for your plan and to measure results.
- A tentative timetable for action.
- An estimate of the resources needed and how they will be obtained.
- Risks and actions to avoid or reduce risks.
- Outline of the organization of the project.

The strategy need not be a detailed plan because, given the various ways projects can be approached, given the variability of resources available, and given the sometimes conflicting and changing interests of the parties to the effort, it will be useful to walk around the problem several times, to see it from different points of view, and to make trade-offs before arriving at an optimal approach that is likely to succeed. So flexibility is important until the strategy has been tested. It is important as well to be willing to work with approximate data. If you insist too soon on overly precise data for market, technical, or accounting analyses, you might spend a great deal of time needlessly. The firm planning and more precise data comes later after you have tested the strategy and are ready to get into detailed planning and action.

Creating strategy has political and psychological dimensions. Reach out and engage people in the creative act of generating a strategy so they will be truly on board when it comes to carrying it out. This can often be done relatively quickly. Small group work sessions can do the trick, sometimes in a few hours and sometimes in a few days.

Be ready for surprises, however. The strategy you have in mind when you start might turn into something quite different when you incorporate your team's points of view. What the group buys into will be more likely to succeed than your original idea would have been if you'd simply pushed it through.

Execution, Plain and Simple

Here is an example of successful strategy development at the operating department level, one beginning with a small group and evolving into a strategy engaging a full department in a few months.

Charlie, manager of an Operations Department in a financial services company, had a clear charge from his boss to reduce the cost of quality across the whole Operations organization by 50 percent in three months. Charlie and his boss agreed Charlie had to create a strategy that people would own and feel confident they could make work.

Charlie pulled together a core team for a two-day work session to develop what he hoped would be a complete plan for the project. He selected a supervisor from his own group, the manager of each of the other five units in Operations, the head of Quality Assurance, the IT representative, the HR representative, and the internal Organization Development consultant.

He presented a five-part agenda—goals, action plan and assignments, measurements, management of the project, and a plan for communications to people in Operations. Most of the people coming into the meeting thought the job would be easy. They'd be able to come up with a detailed plan in just one day. Little did they know what they were getting into.

Getting into the first agenda item for the first morning—the goal—they soon discovered the task was far more complex than anticipated. Each unit had its own interpretation of the cost of quality data, and different ways of using the data in appraising performance. Each had its own view of the best way to reduce the cost of quality. Soon the white board in the conference room was filled with proposed goals, dozens of issues, half a dozen different approaches, but little consensus.

Several times during the morning, Charlie tried to get closure on just a goal, but the definition soon slipped away because different aspects of the definition of cost of quality kept cropping up. People in the core team just were not yet ready to converge on a goal or course of action.

By midafternoon Charlie was frustrated that so little progress had been made. He shifted gears. The aim of getting a complete plan in two days seemed unrealistic. He'd have to settle for something else.

He proposed, instead of a departmentwide effort, one small-scale experiment he felt had a good chance of success. He could set it up in a few days and run a trial of the approach for a month in his own group. At the end of the month, they would have enough experience to know whether his approach would be viable. If so, they could roll out similar plans in other areas. If not, they could then select and test other approaches.

The rest of the meeting was spent on a timetable for key steps for Charlie's experiment, the communication messages, and the data reporting to be provided to Charlie's group. The core team agreed to reconvene in two weeks to review progress and work further on the departmentwide challenge.

There is no one right strategy for change. In this case, the big goal—50-percent reduction in the cost of quality—had to be approached with a small experiment in one unit, followed by engagement of all other unit managers in similar steps. These evolved over a three-month period to a full-scale effort to get to the final goal. In other cases, when there is more consensus, larger scale programs can be conceived.

It is almost always helpful to use a small core team to help create the strategy and then to drive the action. The team makes it easier to address the psychological and political issues, as well as the technical matters of how best to operate. But having a team doesn't mean that the leader abdicates; the leader's job is to drive the whole process.

One-Page Summary

Once you have a strategy in hand, boil it down into a one-page summary. A one-page strategy summary will tell you a lot about whether an issue has really been thought through. A 10-page summary of all the issues, options, and possible plans, and all the risks and countervailing actions, might be impressive to an academic audience, but it is not as convincing as a one-page statement that is clear, easily understood, and explainable in plain language to an average listener. A good strategic summary tells the story about what is going to happen. It is interesting and even exciting. It illustrates a solution to the problem or issue being addressed, outlining the goal, how it is measured, the major actions to be taken, the timetable and the people and resources to be used, and the kind of change to be produced. And that is all that you need at this stage. The strategic summary will form the basis for the next step—testing the strategy with the key people.

Here are the key documents used in the Cost of Quality Reduction project—the invitation, agenda for the strategy meeting, and the one-page summary.

Execution, Plain and Simple

Invitation to the Strategy Meeting
for Reducing Cost of Quality

From: Charlie

To: [Core team, by name]

Subject: Strategy and Agenda for Cost of Quality Strategy Meeting

I'd like to meet with you on Monday and Tuesday August 25–26. Please set the days aside to help deal with a critical issue facing the department. I have been asked by Doug L. [Charlie's boss and sponsor of the project.] to pull together a plan for reducing cost of quality 50 percent in the next three months.

This challenge is necessitated by the reduction in business volume and the need to reduce all costs. Recent data suggests that we should be able to reduce the cost of quality substantially. Over the past two years we have made great strides improving overall quality performance. Having made that investment and seen the results, Doug and I believe we can shift our approach to quality substantially and save money without losing ground on our quality performance.

The question is how best to do this, and how to do it effectively in each of our groups. That's the question we must address together. Please do some thinking about this. Bring your own quality and cost of quality data to the meeting.

Call me if you have questions or issues to discuss before we get together.

Proposed Agenda for the Strategy Meeting
on Reducing Cost of Quality

1. Briefings:
   - Introduction: the assignment and how the assignment was developed.
   - Background data on the department's overall cost of quality and quality performance.
2. Work sessions to get everyone's input and to agree on a plan:
   - The goal and how we'll measure success;
   - How we'll go about this task—the action plan for making the changes needed;
   - Assignments to do the work;
   - Timetable;
   - Communication messages to our people;
   - Schedule for progress reviews.

Organize Your Core Team and Create a Strategy

One-Page Strategy Summary
Reducing Cost of Quality Project

To: Doug

From: Charlie

This project is to reduce the cost of quality in operations by 50 percent in the next three months without negatively affecting actual quality performance.

We're starting with a first test of an approach in my unit only. The following steps will be started now and run for at least a month.

1. Stop weekly inspection and quality assessment of high-performing operators. (We'll use a quarterly audit instead.)
2. Shift quality monitoring responsibility to the work unit from the central QA group, and have a unit supervisor do weekly inspections for lower-performing operators only.
3. Reconfigure the data reporting system so that the quality data is reported directly in the work unit.
4. Keep the few best people from the QA group, and accelerate attrition of poorer-performing operators and QA inspectors to get the cost reduction.

If this works well, we'll implement it in the other groups. We have other options, if needed:

- Eliminating the entire QA group at once
- Focusing on reduction of errors in incoming data (the chief cause of quality problems)
- Renewing the training program to upgrade skills
- Increasing automation of quality inspection and reporting
- Reorganizing the department to build closer ties to major customers and marketing groups in place of the existing functional specialization structure.

Our team [named again here] will be meeting every two weeks to carry out the project. We'd like to have a formal progress review with you in four weeks.

To help you organize your core team and create your strategy, you can use the following worksheets as guidelines.

WORKSHEET:

Selecting and Organizing the Core Team

List the people you want to work with you as a core team for your effort.

_____

_____

_____

Test your list against the criteria for selection of a core team:

- *Competence:* They each know something about the job to be done and can possibly lead a part of the effort.
- *Influence:* They can gain access and have a credible impact on some part of the organization or its stakeholder group.
- *Availability:* They can have time and energy to dedicate to the effort.
- *Representative:* They are part of and can speak for specific constituents.
- *Loyalty:* They are aligned with you and have a sense of responsibility to work with you.
- *Candor:* They are open and willing to share their views, and you trust them enough to listen to them.

How and when will you engage your core team?

_____

_____

_____

Whose support will you need to get them assigned?

_____

_____

_____

How will you get that support?

_____

_____

_____

WORKSHEET:

Strategy Formulation

(This is also an outline for a one-page summary)

- The goal to be achieved and target date for getting the end result.

_____

_____

_____

- The major actions to be taken to reach the goal.

_____

_____

_____

- The people to be involved.

_____

_____

_____

- Relevant data to establish the case for your plan and to measure results.

_____

_____

_____

Execution, Plain and Simple

- A tentative timetable for action.

  _____

  _____

  _____

- An estimate of the resources needed and how they will be obtained.

  _____

  _____

  _____

- Risks and actions to avoid or reduce risks.

  _____

  _____

  _____

- Organization of the project: Leader, core team, other teams/individuals to be involved.

  _____

  _____

  _____

4

Get Input and Support from Key Players; Refine the Strategy

Confident as you might be of your strategy, chances are there are other opinions that matter. It is easy to forget some of the players, but that means bypassing the opportunity to get help from them or to get real problems out of the way. Now that you have a strategy, test it before going into detailed planning and action. For small and relatively straightforward projects, this might take just a few hours. For larger-scale and more complex efforts, it might take days, or even weeks.

Testing the strategy will provide many benefits:

- You will identify the key players and entities involved in or affected by the project, along with their interests in and reactions to the initiative.
- You will find out about substantive issues that need to be addressed and about changes in approach that might be needed for success.
- You will generate interest in the project and readiness to help with it.

Testing, in short, develops understanding and interest that increase your chances of success. It lets you adjust your strategy to take advantage of new insights—both for practical improvements and for smoothing out possible negative or competitive reactions and any other hurdles that crop up during the test. As a result, you will find it much easier to execute your assignment effectively.

The Testing Process

There are four key steps in the testing process:

1. Map the players and processes affected, well beyond your core team, right to the very end.
2. Get in touch with the people on your map to learn their points of view, to identify their issues, and to begin to enlist their support.
3. Summarize your findings.
4. Adjust your strategy.

Map the Players

List as many people and organizations as possible in the following categories:

- Who needs to do the work and help carry out the plan?
- Who—inside and outside the organization—will be affected by it in ways that might change what they are doing?
- Who needs to approve the plan?
- Who will have to put up resources?
- Which outside suppliers will be involved?
- Who are the customers?
- What governmental or regulatory bodies might have an interest?

Reach Out and Establish Contact

Next, establish contact with people on your map. This requires some thought because the way you approach people influences their response. You want to elicit objective, thoughtful, and helpful reactions, without stirring up unnecessary concerns and anxieties—or unrealistic enthusiasm. To do that, state your proposition, but also recognize the recipient's point of view and consider the recipient's interests.

Enlisting support is not at all the same as selling an idea or spinning a problem. Passive acceptance, or even a buying or voting decision, won't be enough from many of the people on your map; you need their active participation. This means exploring the action implications of your strategy for the recipient. It means helping deal with the issues the recipient will face. It might mean changing your strategy in some respects. That's all right. The whole point is to weave an increasingly powerful strategy that anticipates and deals constructively with all the issues to be resolved on the way to achieving the goal. Give-and-take is inevitable.

The testing process can include any or all of the following measures:

- E-mail memos to key people with requests for replies.
- Conversations with key individuals to share your strategy *and to listen to their reactions.* Make notes so the ideas are not lost or distorted later on.
- Meetings with small groups of people representing various interests, for the same purposes.
- Visits to remote sites, to customers and to suppliers as appropriate, to get their views.
- Surveys to reach larger numbers of people expeditiously.

Some Questions to Be Addressed in the Testing Process

What are your overall reactions to the proposed strategy? What is best about it? Worst? Your general sense of how to proceed?

What issues need to be addressed to assure success?

What contribution can you make? What are the implications of these actions for you? How can they be addressed? What help might you need?

What role would you like to play? How can you best relate to or work with this effort?

Summarize

Summarize the reactions you've obtained, starting with the major areas of agreement It is important to highlight these areas of agreement so that people don't get overly preoccupied with their differences. Next, list substantive issues that will need resolution, such as availability of supplies, capacity of support entities to help, items that will require long lead times, conflicting schedules that obstruct progress, technical and policy issues, and organizational and human relations issues.

Adjust Your Strategy

Inevitably the summary will reveal a need for some changes—shifts in goal and scope, adjustments in sequencing of action, additional elements to be added, and other elements to be deleted. Insofar as feasible, all participants should see their ideas and interests advanced, so they can see the reshaped project as a win. Most important, the testing process provides your crystal ball, a look into what you can expect to encounter as the project unfolds. Armed with this insight, you can make adjustments early in the process before you've invested too much in a low-payoff strategy and before you've created so much commitment that it will be difficult to change downstream. With the adjustments, you have heightened your chances for successful execution.

Strategy Testing in Practice

Let's look at an example of how this process works.

Ralph, a supervising engineer in a large electronics manufacturer, was charged by the General Manager of his Division to accelerate completion of his new product. The basic product development cycle in the company at that time consisted of design, prototype build, and test, all done in Engineering. When the design was done, Engineering would "throw it over the transom," believing its job was essentially finished—unless problems arose that might require consultation, and perhaps changing the design or upgrading some features. Then Manufacturing, Quality, Marketing, and Distribution would pick up their responsibilities for seeing the product through to the marketplace. Representatives of all the functions would meet periodically in new product reviews to track progress.

This had been a proven process, deeply embedded in the organization, but at the time of this project, the process was subject to question. The company was under pressure to generate new products much more rapidly. This had to be done with far fewer downstream problems, quality glitches, manufacturing problems, marketing errors, uncoordinated product launches, or regulatory difficulties, any of which would hold up final steps needed to get into the market, meet competitors, and generate revenue.

Ralph was not surprised to be called upon to accelerate completion of this product. It had been his baby from the start. He and his team had conceived the product, designed it, and were nearly ready to go. Vibration problems were unresolved, but he thought he and his team could overcome them in a few weeks and hand the product over to manufacturing without too much more delay. In another sense he was shocked. Bill M., the GM, called upon Ralph to take responsibility from beginning to end, meaning getting the product into the market and generating revenue. This was a vast expansion of his scope of responsibility. All the nonengineering matters had been the job of the various downstream functions. And sister divisions handled the sales, delivery, and service. Now he had to influence all of them to meet *his* overall schedule. This was a whole new ball game.

In a meeting of the top 50 managers of the division, the GM explained that Ralph would be acting with the authority of the General Manager and was expected to see that the product was launched successfully in the market. All the functions were expected to support Ralph. Yes, this was a change. Yes, it was an experiment. But there was no choice. Too many delays and costs were being encountered because of lack of adequate coordination of the downstream activities in the overall new product development process. That had to change. And this project was the starting point for the change. One person was to take prime responsibility for driving the whole project and shortening the cycle at the same time. Ralph would be the pioneer, and he was commissioned to create whatever innovations were needed to produce better results. And on-time product launch was a new expectation—no, a new requirement—a result that counted just as much as meeting technical and quality and cost specs for the product.

Back in this office after the announcement meeting, Ralph was perplexed. How should he tackle this new assignment? He met with the change consultant working with the division on its improvement efforts. The consultant suggested mapping the process and players to be involved as a next step and then to meet with the key people to test his strategy for the project. Together they sat down and drew charts as best they could of each of the processes of new product development and commercialization, the functions involved from beginning to end, the key people and decision makers in each, some of the crucial issues each would have to deal with to do their part, and the problems that might be encountered. They also sketched out a structure for the project—Ralph as the prime leader, with a core team made up of the most crucial functional people who would need to be involved and could serve as ambassadors from the project to their respective functional organizations. They listed the anticipated issues, and some of the problems, and a broad view of how the project might proceed—a tentative strategy.

Execution, Plain and Simple

Next, they walked through the division and met with the heads of each of the functions, one to one, to show their charts and issues lists and tentative strategy and ask for reactions. Ralph was somewhat surprised that he had done a good job mapping the processes, players, and issues. The other managers made just a few modifications, suggesting some additional people for the core team. He was more surprised by their attitude. It was far more positive than he had expected. Each felt the experiment was a good step to take and that Ralph and this product were good candidates for this kind of experiment. "Just tell us what you want us to do. And we'll be ready to go. But do it soon." They explained a number of competing forces that would consume their time and energy. Many other new products were coming down the pipeline. The Circuit Board group was seriously behind schedule and was understaffed. A new CAD-CAM system was being installed and tested and was far from debugged. Marketing thought that some customers would want design changes and certainly some price reductions.

Back in his office again, Ralph now had a new view of the job to be done. He could see that that vibration engineering would be the least of his problems. He couldn't commit to a completion date without getting all the functions to buy into a date *they* could also meet. And he had to figure out a way to manage this total group even though they had plenty to do and were still party to the regular ongoing product reviews. He wondered where he would get the resources to deal with some of the tougher problems like Circuit Board Department overload and staffing, the possible design modifications, the CAD-CAM glitches, and the needed cost reductions.

Ralph decided to call a meeting of a new proposed core team to discuss these issues and to get agreement on a new time line and target date for product launch. He shared the results of his "test" of his original strategy and outlined the new views he had developed encompassing some of the problems he had heard about in his discussions. With some discussion, the new core team reached agreement on a time line and target date.

Too often this kind of mapping process is skipped over lightly or omitted entirely. Many of the problems of execution can be traced directly to this oversight. It is easy to blame people or fate when issues seem to pop out of nowhere to confound a project, or resistance arises in unexpected quarters. Chances are, however, that the initiators could have anticipated these difficulties and done more to accommodate them if they had adequately tested their strategy with key people in advance.

Mapping the Players

The mapping worksheet at the end of this chapter provides a tool to gather and organize the insights about readiness and other factors affecting project strategy. You can list the various players. For each you can indicate reactions. In addition, you can indicate what specific actions are needed to deal with the issues raised by each constituent.

Keep in mind that this is a dynamic process. People change their minds. Interaction leads to new perceptions of what can and cannot be done. Energy ebbs and flows as ideas seem to fall apart and then suddenly gel. This kind of testing is not a cut-and-dried process intended to create a strategy once and for all. It is a process for sharpening your approach, for enlisting allies, and for generating motivation to act and to act cooperatively. It is a process for increasing the chances for success. So stay loose. Use pencil and paper—not indelible ink—when drawing your map and doing your testing.

WORKSHEET:

Mapping

 Mapping the Players

Constituency/Names	Reactions of the Players	Issues/Action to be Taken
Direct Participants		
Indirect Participants		
Others Affected		
Policy/Financial/Approvers		
Suppliers		
Customers		
Regulators		
Others		

© RHS&A 2003

Act with Discipline

5

Hold a Compelling Kickoff Event to Create Momentum

Once you have a tested strategy, launch it. Depending on the scope, a short meeting might be enough, but you might want a working session of a half-day or full day, or even a conference that pulls people together for several days.

The launch event defines the transition from strategy formulation to action. It assembles all the key players to:

- Review and sharpen the strategy to ensure common understanding and acceptance.
- Shape the master plan and set key milestone dates.
- Define the measures of success and the measurement process.
- Create specific assignments and work plans.
- Get people to commit themselves to their part of the work.
- Define the follow-up management process.
- Allocate resources to the tasks to be done.
- Set dates for the next progress review events.

- Prepare a message to all parties involved or affected by the effort, summarizing the decisions and actions taken at the launch event.

Why do you need a kickoff event? It takes a special effort to get people's attention and to do something new. A well-run launch event generates a shift—a signal of real change—that is an essential ingredient of effective execution.

The event should be something special. Give it a sense of drama and make a real effort to generate energy and commitment to coordinated action. You want some argument, not just hoopla; intense dialogue in the meeting flushes out assumptions, clarifies understanding of what's to be done, and builds mutual understanding so that people grasp the whole effort, their own roles, and know how to stay in touch with and interact with others.

If you'll need an OK from higher in the organization to proceed with your strategy, get it before the launch—but don't confuse a decision meeting with a launch meeting. In a launch meeting you have all the key players in the room, conducting a deep-down, intensive dialogue to assure solid mutual understanding of the strategy, the plan, the roles and responsibilities, and the action assignments—all the issues relevant to successful execution. The genuine clarity and commitment all relevant people have coming out of the meeting is the mark of a successful launch event.

Preparation

Figure 5-1 provides an overview of what you need to consider to plan a successful launch event.

Prepare an agenda and invitation list. To plan the agenda, start at the end—visualize people presenting to you and the full group how they will move ahead. Picture the communiqué you'll want to issue at the end of the launch event. Then work back to the beginning of the meeting and allocate blocks of time to the various pieces of work to be done:

- Present the charge and strategy.
- Answer questions and discuss reactions to get agreement.

Hold a Compelling Kickoff Event to Create Momentum

Launch Events

- Get people together
- Generate plans and commitments
- Signal a shift from planning to action
- Create energy
- Create control

Plan Your Launch Event

- Do you need one?
- What is the agenda?
- Who will be invited?
- How will you prepare?
- What help will you use?
- What will be the facility/logistics?

Launch Event Do's and Don'ts

Do	Don't
Invite "right" people—all key players and support and others who will help	Invite people to audit and who will have no active role
Prepare agenda—for presentation, work session, feedback	Overdo work or fun—get a balance
Use facilitation help	Skimp on preparation
Pay attention to facilities and logistics	Treat logistics and facilities as trivial issues

Figure 5-1. Launch Event Planning

- Shape the master plan, measurements and timetable for accomplishment.
- Carve out subpieces and prepare preliminary work plans for these, keyed to the master plan.
- Review subordinate work plans with the group to assure that they fit together. (Allow time for resolution of issues.)
- Decide on the management process
- Wrap up and develop the final communiqué.

List the people you believe must attend. You want your core team members, the leaders of each subproject, and people from related functions that will need to interact with the effort, along with key staff to provide data, technical support, or direct assistance. Sometimes it is useful to invite end users, customers, or suppliers as well. They can provide important insight and help downstream. Ask your boss and appropriate senior leaders of the company to attend the opening of the meeting and provide a management perspective, emphasizing the place of this effort in the organization's overall strategy and work program. The same leaders should attend the conclusion of the event to hear how people plan to move ahead, help resolve remaining issues, and provide support as appropriate.

Choose a good facility for your meeting. Believe it or not, the room makes a big difference. A room for a meeting of 20 or 30 people has to be big enough for 20 or 30 people, with some space to walk around, space off to the side, and a place for coffee and soft drinks. Cramped facilities cramp the flow of the meeting; overlarge ones embarrass the participants and make them wonder where the other people who should be there have gone—and what made them stay away. Noisy air conditioners, raucous groups in neighboring rooms separated only by a thin partition, dim lighting, lack of white boards, irrelevant charts from other meetings, all will distract people and detract from the meeting. Make sure you line up a place suited to the work at hand.

Send the invitations with the agenda and preparation assignments for the participants.

Assemble your materials—all the basic elements of your program: the initial charge, the strategy you've developed, the data that helps make the case for the effort and spells out the desired results and their impact on the organization. Bring your sketch of the master plan and the major assignments you have in mind, along with the kind of measurements and the management and review process you want, and some proposed dates for key events and progress reviews. But, again, be flexible. The whole purpose of the launch is to generate energy, ideas, and commitment, and that requires creative input from the group. No matter how good your strategy, you need to be open to new insights that generate better ways to proceed.

If this seems to be too much to do in one meeting, then break it up and schedule several sessions to work on parts.

Consider getting help from an outside facilitator. Of course, you need direct and thorough communication among the group, and bringing in a third party might seem likely to interfere with this essential process. But consider these issues carefully:

- *Would you be able to keep everyone—including yourself—on track and on schedule?* Launch meetings tend to wander beyond the agenda, getting into side issues or protracted debates better resolved elsewhere, but that's very hard to see while you're taking part in the extraneous discussion.
- *How would you cope when people seem to reach a dead end or get into conflicts?* A third party can see things from a different perspective and help resolve issues, or suggest new ways to proceed.
- *Would you be sure to hear from everyone?* Some people are aggressive and tend to dominate any gathering. Others hang back—even though they often have some of the most valuable things to say. Someone with no prior ties to the participants can help stimulate and balance the discussion to assure that all parties are heard and participate effectively.

If you're certain you can run the meeting and take part in it productively at the same time, go for it. Make your own plan for dealing with the three issues of focus, conflict resolution, and participation. But the larger and more difficult the meeting and the more you care about the outcome, the more you should consider enlisting expert assistance from staff people, other managers who are sensitive to the issues of group processes, or an outside expert.

Execution, Plain and Simple

Make it fun. People will need a light touch to balance the heavy-duty work involved. Breaks. Some special presentations, a game or two, good food, sports events, walks around the conference site—all help rejuvenate participants. Don't go too far, though. Here's a case where the facilitator might have gone too far:

> The facilitator handed out soft plastic balls and airplanes at the beginning, saying, "This is going to be a fun event!" Well, when things got a little slow, people grew bored, and the planes and balls began to fly. Some people were favorite targets of others. If a presenter was turning people off, the room turned into a virtual battle zone with objects flying in all directions. Not a word was said. The flow of toys told its own story, not only of the mood of the meeting but of the underlying tensions and rivalries among the participants as well. The meeting was reasonably successful, but the by-play suggested it could have been better. There was no by-play when the discussions were important and everyone was engaged.

Check out the meeting site well in advance and make sure it is set up with the right table configuration to suit the meeting. Auditorium style is all right for a speech or a classroom, but not for a working launch meeting. Arrange tables in a U or a square so people can see and talk with one another. Or set up cafeteria style where subteams can sit at tables together for their work sessions on their own plans and still participate in the full group proceedings.

Plan also to overcome the distractions people bring with them. In this multitasking world, armed with cell phones, wireless computers, PDAs, pagers, and IM devices, people are accustomed to working and thinking and responding to dozens of issues simultaneously. Your meeting doesn't stand a chance in this environment. You want complete attention to the task, but you'll be lucky to get 20 percent if you don't deal with this issue up front. Set ground rules. All phones, computers, and pagers off. Allow time for phone breaks instead. If people are likely to have urgent calls or problems to deal with during the meeting, see if alternative arrangements can be made. Refer the calls to someone else, take time out to resolve issues before a call comes, or just go on without the people who can't really participate effectively even though they might have a real place in the effort. Find another way to get them involved. Constant interruptions undermine deliberations. On the other hand, recognize that very busy people are often the most effective people, so make the meeting fast and compelling. The distractions might melt away if you get people properly engaged.

A Basic Full-Day Launch Event

Picture yourself looking in a dimly lit conference room in a factory in northern Mexico. The product: cardboard boxes, boxes used primarily by sister companies in a large conglomerate—a brewery, soap maker, and other manufacturers.

The plant management team assembles for an important meeting. The problem is waste—and waste is obvious all over the factory. Raw fiberboard is stored in an open yard, subject to rain, sun, and constantly changing humidity. Much of it is curled or torn. The plant floor is strewn with scraps and stacks of partly used material. Piles of work in process crowd the aisles and the Shipping Department. Dumpsters of waste sit next to the shipping dock.

The plant manager speaks some English. The others on the team, representing all the key functions of the plant, speak only Spanish. The only other person in the room is an American consultant—equipped with just rudimentary high-school Spanish but plenty of wisdom about waste reduction. The plant manager opens the meeting by introducing the people and the consultant and presents a 15-minute monologue on the job to be done. Then he turns to the consultant. "I told them we are here to reduce waste. Everyone agrees we need to do it. What do we do next?"

The consultant says simply, "Pick a goal. How much do you want to reduce waste, and when?" (He had discovered the day before, touring the plant, that the managers already had plenty of ideas and know-how about waste reduction. They had done many studies. The real challenge was to generate coordinated action to do something about it, and he was sure that his standard presentation about waste reduction had no place in this room.)

The plant manager nods, turns to his group, and talks for 10 minutes in animated Spanish. Then the group pitches in. One man runs out and returns shortly with a sheaf of papers. Everyone crowds around to look at rows of numbers. A lot of animated argument begins. After an hour of this discussion, the manager goes to the board and writes down two numbers: the number of pounds of waste per week to be reduced, and a time period, two months. Discussion quiets.

He turns to the consultant. "We have a goal and a date. Now what do we do?"

"Appoint a project leader. Write the name on the board."

The process repeats, with more animated discussion. Soon a name is printed in large script on the board. While one fellow squirms, the others smile or look away with some embarrassment. "Now what do we do?"

"List the steps to be taken, by whom—a work plan."

The plant manager takes a long drink of water; the monologue resumes, and then more debate. Gradually, over more than another hour, items appear on the board—with a name next to each. By the end it is clear that everyone in the room has a piece of the action, and the board is nearly full of things to do to reduce waste and achieve the goal.

The consultant interjects quietly, "Now let's ask the project leader to write up the schedule for progress review meetings he'll have with this team, and how and when he'll report back to you that the goal is achieved."

The plant manager resumes the meeting and after more discussion the designated leader gets up and draws a calendar on the last remaining space on the board. He fills in X's for the dates for the reviews and the final report—everyone nods.

"What's next?" asks the plant manager.

"Ask everyone how they feel about what you have accomplished. Will this plan work?"

The ritual resumes, this time with more excitement in the air. "*Jugando.* Now we're playing together!"

The consultant uttered only five sentences in a meeting that ran almost all day, but set a lot of change in motion with those few words.

It's as simple as that. When a manager has an objective, brings together the people who can help, and has a sense of what needs to be accomplished, it doesn't take a lot of words to crystallize a direction and get change started. By contrast, lectures, edicts, and ambiguous suggestions are often smokescreens that pass as management discourse about changes to be made. They allow their perpetrators to sound like they're taking action when they are not.

The group at the box factory had more work to do to see things through to successful completion. Nonetheless, the meeting illustrates the basic elements of a launch event and some basic principles:

- To get started, state the change to be made in a very few words.
- Answer at least the five key questions for any initiative:
  1. What's the goal?
  2. Who is the leader and core team?
  3. What's the plan?
  4. How will success be measured and reported?

5. How do people feel about what they are doing?

Of course, this isn't the only way for a launch meeting to go. For a small project, you might be able to cover the ground with half a dozen people in your office; for a plantwide initiative, it might take a hundred people offsite for several days. If you're thinking about a big and complex project and need to engage people who normally are not engaged adequately, consider the Work-Out process, which was developed at General Electric as a device to stimulate widespread creative action to improve productivity, speed, and self-confidence throughout the company. GE has used it as an almost universal launch event for hundreds of different situations, and many other organizations have picked up on it. (For more information, see *The GE Work-Out,* by Dave Ulrich, Steve Kerr, and Ron Ashkenas.)

Whatever you do to launch your project, take the time to think it through in advance. The following is a sample worksheet you can use to plan your kickoff.

WORKSHEET:

Planning a Launch Event

1. Format:

   Informal meeting: _____

   Formal on-site meeting:_____

   Off-site gathering: _____

2. Participants (list individual names, plus other groups to be invited to send representatives):

   _____

   _____

   _____

---

3. Agenda and timetable:
   a. Introductions and purpose.
   b. Review the challenge to be addressed, the data, and the preliminary strategy.
   c. Group reactions, and then brainstorming as needed on how to respond to the challenge.
   d. Select best ideas and layout out a master plan, measurements, and timetable.
   e. Form action teams to tackle the major parts of the master plan, and sketch their assignments and initial actions.
   f. Review proposed action plans for adequacy and coordination.
   g. Communication messages.
   h. Management Process: Follow-up steps and schedule for progress reviews.

4. Preparation required:

   _____

   _____

   _____

5. Facilitation:

   _____

   _____

   _____

6. Site and logistical planning:

   _____

   _____

   _____

6

Make All the Pieces Fit. Use Plans, Schedules, Budgets, and Controls

Coming out of the launch event, you'll have your team charged up and moving. You might still have some issues to resolve and some aspects of the effort to clear up. But you'll have your goal, major elements of your plan, your management process, teams starting to work, and things should be heading in the right direction.

One of the keys to keeping everyone moving forward, doing what needs to be done and coordinating their efforts, is to spell out the specific tasks in writing. People need to know what has to be completed, when, by whom; how work in one area is supposed to connect with and support work in other areas; how the connections will take place; where help can be found; and where and how issues can be resolved.

This is where the detailed work plan comes into play. The written work plan is the principal tool for guiding action and managing execution. It spells out the essentials in very specific detail. For any program, this means:

- The goal and the target date for its achievement.
- The overall master plan—major streams of action, substreams, and milestone dates for key elements.
- The accountable overall leader and leaders for each piece of the plan.
- The specific steps to be taken, by whom, and when for each piece of the plan.
- The measurements and indicators of project success.
- The progress review and coordination events.
- The resources of money and people and how and when they will be applied.
- Sources of help and how they can be accessed.

In other words, the project work plan is a road map. It provides an orderly guide for channeling all the team's energy toward the goal and lining up the resources to support the effort so the plan can be executed successfully.

You might wonder at what point detailed planning is best done. For well-understood, repeated, and relatively fixed undertakings such as some manufacturing, financing, and construction activities, detailed planning early in the process is appropriate. The factors are well known in advance or predictable. High efficiency and tight control are vital for success. In situations where people are attuned to orderly and highly structured work, a detailed plan in advance is needed to make clear what is expected and to reduce the discomfort of uncertainty.

In situations where there is more rapid change and high uncertainty, flexibility and improvisation are much more vital to success than high efficiency and tight control. Too much advanced planning can be a waste of time, or even an impediment to success. In these situations, planning for accomplishment of a goal is really evolving at every stage of the execution process. There is some degree of planning evident in the strategy, and more is developed in the launch event. But the really detailed planning is done much closer to the actual action events, by the people directly involved, almost as the action is happening.

Make All the Pieces Fit

In any case, putting the plan on paper is an exercise in thinking things through. The leader and core team develop the master plan and define major subplans. As the effort gets moving, more people are involved in shaping the specific action for subplans so that they are not academic documents but something people understand, own, and follow. The level of detail and comprehensiveness needed in the plan depend on the size and complexity of the job to be done, the precision required for successful execution, the familiarity of the people with the work to be done, and their experience working together. For work that is very familiar and routine, a very simple plan suffices. Sometimes a one- or two-page work plan is all that is needed to manage a simple project, keep the team on track, and communicate to the boss and others. But more complex projects require much more extensive planning. Construction of a large building, computer system, or dam can require war rooms full of plans and highly sophisticated reporting and tracking systems for all the pieces and subpieces of work to be done.

The things you need to do to construct a good plan, regardless of size and complexity, are fairly straightforward.

- Define the goal, target date, and measures of success.
- Define the steps to be taken. Make the plan comprehensive and complete, covering all the steps that can be foreseen.
- Sequence the steps so that no piece of the plan is held up for lack of completion of another piece.
- Call for each step when it is needed, not before.
- Start early with long-lead-time items because they are the determining factor in the time cycle of the plan.
- Do as much as possible in parallel to maximize the speed and efficiency of completion.
- Make the work plan reflect realistic commitments to deliver, not assumptions about what people ought to be able do and when. Test this commitment—and test it hard—before committing the step to writing as part of the plan. (A plan developed without commitment of the players is a template, more than a plan.)
- Provide for orientation and integration of new team members. You can't always count on getting all the players involved up front.

Some won't even have been recruited for the job when the plans are drawn, so make sure you plan for effective orientation and education to bring new people on board and show them how to do their part.

- Build in risk-reduction steps to reduce the likelihood of errors and delays.
- Back up the main plan with contingency plans to cope with what might go wrong, and hedge risky items with plenty of flexibility to allow for the delays or faults that might occur.
- Provide for sources and amounts of money (budget) and people (staffing), and other resources specifying how much is needed of each and when.
- Specify progress review and coordination events.
- Specify sources of help.
- Build and distribute rosters of the people involved with their phone, e-mail, and fax numbers.

Work back from the end point. That is, visualize the end result—successful completion. Then ask, what would happen right before the final success? Right before that? It takes several, sometimes many, iterations of this thought process to generate all the steps back to the beginning—where you are now—and to fully sequence the steps for the plan.

For complex plans, you can use planning tools such as PERT and GANTT charts or computerized planning tools to document the thinking. Figure 6-1 summarizes the key ingredients to consider in the planning process.

Controls

The plan is essentially a device to establish control of human activity and harness it to your objective. The plan maps out what needs to be done. People make commitments to do what they are asked to do under the plan. The plan is the foundation for control.

Control steps are needed to gauge how work is actually progressing, the results being achieved, and the resources being used. The simplest and most direct control mechanism is the report of someone acting on a

---

Major Elements of a Plan

- The goal and the target date for its achievement.

- The overall master plan—major actions and their objectives and milestone dates, subactions and their objectives, and milestone dates for key elements.

- The accountable overall leader and leaders for each piece of the plan.

- The specific steps to be taken, by whom, and when for each subpiece of the plan.

- The measurements and indicators of project success.

- The progress review and coordination events.

- The resources of money and people and how and when they will be applied.

- Sources of help and how they will be accessed.

Figure 6-1. Elements of a Plan

step in the plan. This can be done informally day by day. It can be done more rigorously (and it should be done rigorously) in periodic progress review meetings and at meetings at key junctures of the project.

The level of control needed depends on the stakes at issue. In a submarine, for example, where everything is a matter of life and death, all action is very tightly controlled. Every order is repeated aloud and confirmed before being carried out, and every action is checked to confirm the desired effect. Few business decisions require that level of precision, but you have to keep in touch with progress to be sure of getting the results you need for successful execution.

Written reports of progress against the work plan, or weekly or monthly written progress reports, can serve this purpose.

A monthly operations review meeting is perhaps the most powerful mechanism for keeping everyone on track with the overall goal and the main elements of the plan. The overall project leader reviews the original goal and major plan elements. The subteam leaders each report progress on their part of the plan. The overall leader posts her results against the master plan. When everything is moving on plan, reviews can be quite brief; people check in and then go back to their own segments of the work. But discrepancies are inevitable, and that makes most major progress reviews a combination of reporting sessions and working sessions. Ideally, differences between planned and actual progress are reported frankly and discussed openly and candidly, and the group generates ideas on ways to catch up on slippages or overcome obstacles ahead. People address coordination issues as they surface. In the process, policy issues and other matters that require off-line study are assigned. Notes are made and distributed on the decisions and actions assigned. The discipline with which these progress reviews are carried out has a profound effect on project success. These sessions are worth doing very well.

Such progress reviews are best done in person. Face-to-face interaction makes the intense communication, reading of body language, and shared understanding much easier to achieve. But dispersed teams can review progress with reasonable effectiveness by telephone or videoconference or virtually by e-mail or direct file sharing—especially when people are familiar with their tasks, know one another, and don't need close interaction to be tuned in. Given the worldwide scope of so many undertakings and the difficulties and cost of travel, electronic communication is the only feasible method.

If the work is dispersed, the leader should make personal site visits to see what is actually happening in various parts of the effort, and to listen to people on the project and get their perceptions of what is happening. The leader should also ask questions of and listen to end customers.

All this walking around and listening does mean "going around" the team leaders and getting information from many sources as well as those directly responsible for carrying out parts of the plan. If you are ultimately responsible for the actions and results of an organization, whether it be a two-person team, a larger team effort, a whole division, or even a company, you do have to verify for yourself that results are really happening according to plan. That is an inherent part of exercising leadership responsibility.

Data Reporting

It is essential to maintain a dashboard of performance data and financial data so that both the leader and the participants can see the effect the effort is having (or not having) on the goal.

Track three basic aspects of your work program: actual performance of the result you're after, progress against the milestones in the master plan, and spending against budget. These categories will let you see how you are doing. If you find that you're off plan on any aspect, pause and take stock—by yourself and with your core team—and decide what is to be done to get back on plan. Sometimes the plan itself needs to be modified—but be cautious about it. Do not adjust the original goal without very good reason, or without agreement from the key parties who established the goal in the first place. In most cases, you'll be ahead of the game if you innovate and find better ways to get back on plan rather than succumb to the temptation to modify it.

Results

Results are what you're trying to get. If your project aims to increase on-stream time of a chemical process, for example, then what you want to measure, track, and report is the actual hours of processing time as a proportion of the total available operating time during a specified period. If it is to reduce errors in insurance claims processing, then—once you have very precise definitions of what constitutes an error—you have the defined errors counted accurately for a given time period and then reported back.

It's a big job to establish and report good measurements. If measurements and reporting processes aren't available, invest the effort to develop them. Most often you will find you have plenty of measurements and plenty of data available, and you just have to sort through to find the data you need.

If the goal is to change the performance variable as compared to prior values, then the historical baseline has to be defined, and that baseline is specified in the reporting charts. Thus if you are trying to reduce claims processing errors to half of what they were last year, obviously you need a number for errors last year—your baseline. If errors weren't being counted properly last year and can't be reconstructed, then you can use the starting value as a baseline instead.

Virtually every human endeavor can ultimately be expressed numerically. All you need is something you can count that varies along with how well you're doing, and a systematic way to decide when to count it—a time interval, number of items produced, or some other measure. If you can't boil down a goal to that level, it's probably a sign that the thinking behind the project is vague, the understanding is superficial, and the results will almost certainly be unsatisfactory. The results chart shown in Figure 6-2 is the primary measurement and reporting tool.

To prepare a results chart, take the following steps:

1. Lay out the time line for your project on the horizontal axis.
2. Lay out measurement increments for the key end result variable on the vertical axis.
3. Draw the past performance level as a baseline on the chart.
4. Draw a diagonal line showing your planned improvement of results from the baseline to the target level over the course of the project.
5. Plot your actual results week by week as the project proceeds.

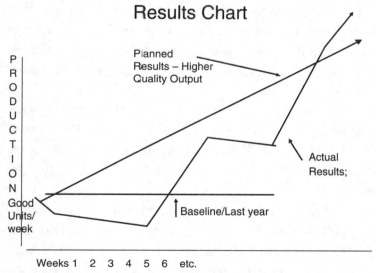

Figure 6-2. Results Chart

6. Post the chart where participants in the project can see it. Distribute copies to all key players.

When you distribute and post your data in this fashion, everyone will quickly see if your effort is really being successful. If "the needle" doesn't move when it should, then that is a clear signal to pause, take stock, learn what is happening, and take corrective action.

Work Program

You also need to track the specific steps being taken in your project plan. The master plan milestone chart shows the main streams of activity and the dates when key steps are to be accomplished. Subordinate work plans specify actions and dates for completion of various pieces of work. The progress report shows the actual accomplishment against the planned milestones. This is the second key factor to follow, using a chart like the one in Figure 6-3.

Here are the steps for plotting a master plan:

1. Plot the time line along the horizontal axis.
2. List the major actions in your master plan and the key milestone points for each at the appropriate place on the time line.
3. Mark the times for key events and progress reviews.
4. Record progress by checking items off on the chart as they are completed, or show a colored line tracking progress against the plan line.

Master Plan Action Chart

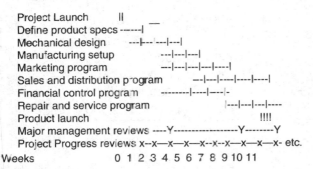

Figure 6-3. Master Plan Action Chart

This type of chart will quickly show you whether or not work is being completed according to plan. As with the results chart, falling behind plan is a signal to pause and find out what is happening—and to take corrective action.

Resources

Then there's the question of actual spending—for people, supplies, and other resources—against the planned or budgeted spending. A report like the one shown in Figure 6-4 is the third segment of the control program.

To prepare the spending chart:

1. List the major spending items in your project budget and the planned spending for each period (usually a week, month, or quarter).
2. Fill in actual spending for each item as the project proceeds, and calculate the amount over and under budget for the period and cumulatively to track actual spending against the plan.

Again, if spending is getting off plan, it is a signal to pause, find out what is happening, and take corrective action.

Budget and Spending Chart

Month	1	2	3	4
Planned spending				
Labor	10,000	10,000	10,000	
Materials	2,000	2,000	2,000	
Services	3,000	3,000	3,000	
TOTAL	15,000	15,000	15,000	etc.
Actual spending				
Labor	10,000	10,000	10,000	
Materials	2,000	2,000	1,000	
Services	3,000	7,000	2,500	
TOTAL	15,000	19,000	13,500	
OverUnder/Month	0	–(4,000)	+1,500	
Total to date	0	–(4,000)	–(2,500)	etc.

Figure 6-4. Spending Chart

By monitoring results, milestones, and resources in this fashion, you can exercise control. The measurement reports will focus your efforts on doing what is necessary to achieve the goal on time and on budget.

Pitfalls of Controls and Plans

It can be tempting to measure everything in sight and add all sorts of bells and whistles to the reporting system. Resist. It's best to keep tracking as simple as possible. Use the measurements and reporting recommended in the preceding section religiously. If the resulting charts are simple, readable, timely, and visible to all who need to know, you and your people are more likely to use them. Without them it is nearly impossible to control any work program of substance and to bring in the results on time and on budget—but bury them in too many more kinds of reports and you might be almost as lost as you would be without them.

Bear in mind that one of the hazards of plan making is that it easily takes on a life of its own. This is especially true when the planning is complex and is handed off to a formal planning group or to consultants. Hours, days, and weeks are spent doing the thinking, doing the calculations, drawing up charts, reviewing them with key people. The objective becomes the development of a perfect plan.

The objective is not to have perfect plans, however, but to have effective action taken by real people dealing with real problems day by day. So don't overinvest in formal planning. Do a general outline of a long-term plan, with the major pieces of work and time lines spelled out as a start. Then do short-range plans—say 30, 60, and 90 days—more specifically, within the longer-term framework. The process of planning and action then has more meaning. Work proceeds, like a football team marching down the field, with a series of huddles and quick plays to move toward the goal. A series of short-range action plans are carried out keyed to the realities immediately ahead, but on the path to the long-term goal, just as the football team builds on its plays to win the game, and, in the longer term, the championship.

Preliminary plans can and generally should be constructed during the kick-off meeting. They'll need to be refined and reworked as events unfold, but it's useful to channel all that early energy into specific action—so people are not just excited about doing something, but about doing something

61

specific, right now, that will feed into the ultimate goal. The following worksheets will assist in the process of long-range and short-range planning.

WORKSHEET:

Long-Term Plan

Sketch out a long-term plan for your project—the goal, major streams of activity, and the time line with major overall milestones.

Goal:_____

_____

_____

Prime Accountable Manager:_____

_____

Major Stream of Action	Manager	Q1 Milestones	Q2 Milestones	Q3 Milestones	Q4, etc.

WORKSHEET:

Short-Term Plan

Pick a short-term segment and sketch a specific work plan

Goal:_____

_____

(Include what will be achieved; how it will be measured; and the target date.)

Team Leader: _____

Team Members: _____

_____

Steps (Start Each with Action Verb)	Person Responsible	Target Dates		Status as of:
		Begin	**End**	

* If more than one person is responsible, circle who has prime responsibility.

7

Yes, I Really Mean It. Make Demands Effectively

The execution steps began with the largely intellectual exercise of framing an assignment, then got into the more political task of shaping a strategy and building a constituency. Next came the theatrical task of running the launch event. And then the technical task of developing plans, schedules, budgets, measurements, and controls.

Throughout this process you have been making demands. You made demands to clarify your assignment. You made demands to assemble your core team and create a strategy. You made demands to carry out a launch event and to create plans. Here we'll look into the whole demand-making process in more depth because it has such a profound effect on success.

The basic impulse that animates the whole process of execution is the human drive for achievement and dominance, in short, the exercise of power. It is this drive that gets things done. It stirs dormant people awake. It pushes wafflers and doubters into advocates. It transforms skeptics into supporters. It diverts or neutralizes opponents. It makes things happen.

The raw exercise of power in modern organizations is taboo, however. Management theory and the human relations movement have sublimated this force, substituting mission, inspiration, dialogue, incentives, and structure as devices to generate productive work. Especially in idea-centric organizations, productive work requires imaginative initiative, cooperative and coordinated action, and self-motivation. The exercise of power is seen as smothering these impulses, so experts cast it aside. They propose instead environments and cultures that foster productive work and let people be free to manage themselves.

Somehow, however, the exercise of power is an enduring reality in any organization, even the most sophisticated. Managers exercise their power by making demands. They translate the need to achieve goals into specific directions to get things done. Effective demand making is essential in managing execution. Managers make demands so people coalesce their energies for accomplishment of a goal. Managers make demands to mobilize people to reach higher goals and to do so on time and on budget. Even in a string quartet, the ultimate collaborative professional and seemingly leaderless organization, the players look to someone for the subtle signals to start the music, to set the tempo, to shape the dynamics. Virtually nothing productive happens in organizations without demands being made in some way. The question for managers is how best to do it.

It is hard to find simple models. At one extreme is the tyrannical manager who drives people and gets cooperation in return for survival in the organization. At the other is the passive and supportive coach, who is a comforting presence but not an animator of action and often leaves people willing to work but unsure of what needs to be done. Reject both extremes.

If you are going to be effective at execution, you'll need to master the fine art of demand making. You'll need to discover how to translate the need to get something done into specific directions as appropriate for each situation.

It is, of course, simplistic to assert only two dimensions of managerial leadership behavior. Effective leadership involves an array of elements: shared values, a clear sense of direction and the discipline to pursue that direction, integrity above all. And a sense of success—people follow leaders for the reasons cited, but also because they discover that the leaders just know how to do things right, how to generate successes. Working with such leaders is a source of strength.

Successful execution requires making demands in ways that generate productive responses. You will really need to call on your demand-making capabilities during the hard work of carrying out the plans. That is when the forces of complexity, inertia, diversion, even opposition assert themselves, and when the strengths of managerial leadership are tested most severely.

Demand Making

There are five aspects of the demand-making process to be understood and practiced:

- Definition
- Presentation
- Personalization
- Preparation
- Closure

If you nail down each of these, you'll mobilize people more effectively and multiply the impact of your own effort.

Clarity

Be clear about what you are demanding. This might seem obvious and trivial—but it is not so easy and certainly not trivial in practice. Picture the frustrated manager who in a meeting fumes, casts blame, threatens, and cajoles, but doesn't really settle on what the staff should do next, in ways that make sense. People leave the meeting flustered and confused and just keep doing what they've been doing because there is no other direction to follow. Or the brilliant and voluble manager who covers everything in endless monologues directed at the team—then leaves it to the team members to sort things out. But their responses are never satisfactory because the manager has not thought things through to the point of being specific about direction and next steps to be taken. Or the manager who almost purposely gives self-protecting, self-contradictory direction, for example, urging people to innovate, but not to make mistakes.

Stop! Think things through. What specifically are you asking people to do? Put it in writing, following the guidelines for good assignments suggested in Chapter 2.

Presentation

Stage the demand. The medium is a big part of the message. Is the demand to be made in a thoughtful, confidential, one-on-one conversation? In a meeting with several others as well? In a written communication? Running down the hall? In a phone call? A phone mail message? An e-mail note? Off site in a lunch or dinner meeting? Put yourself in the recipient's shoes. If you want the recipient to understand, accept, and be committed to responding to the assignment you are giving, what would be the best way to present it?

Personalization

Calibrate the demand to the receiver. No two relationships are the same. While some commonsense guidelines help with demand making in general, effectiveness depends very much on the relationship between the demand maker and the receiver. People who have worked together for years have an enormous history of interaction. Much is mutually understood without being said because of that history. A few words or suggestions can get something new to happen.

People who are ambitious and think of themselves as self-starters and on top of things, might resent a new demand because they interpret it as a comment on their failure to see the issue and act on it before being asked to do so. For these people, a demand might begin with a question rather than a request. Ask, "What do you think of [some issue]?" The recipient's wheels start turning and ideas pour forth while readiness to take some action builds. Simple dialogue can then shape a course of action that makes sense. In this case, the initiator is a partner with the receiver in shaping the demand.

More difficult are the demands that call for someone to do something really different or face up to some deficiencies or set out for a higher goal. Preparation is essential for such discussions. You need to prepare your presentation of the substance of the matter as suggested under the heading of "Definition," of course. But you also need psychological preparation for a discussion that might be stressful for both the demand maker and the receiver.

Preparation

Prepare for the interaction. If demand making were just a matter of conveying a message, it would be relatively easy. But more likely it involves a two-way and dynamic interaction. On receiving the message—or what is perceived as the message—the recipient immediately starts thinking and reacting. What is this? What is really being requested? Why am I getting this assignment now? How can I do this with everything else I have to do? Does this conflict with the assignment I got yesterday, last week? Didn't someone else get the same assignment just last month? Where am I to get help doing this? The demand maker, sensing these reactions, responds to these issues and can easily be drawn off course, get into dialogue responding to one issue or another, and lose track of the main message.

With tougher assignments, such as those that initiate significant change, you're likely to get still more challenging reactions—people will see the request as an outrageous expectation, and many won't be shy about telling you so.

As the demand maker, be prepared in advance to respond to these reactions—on the spot. So some quiet rehearsal can be helpful in preparing for the discussion. One way is to read the assignment you have drafted back to yourself aloud. Does it sound right, making a strong call to action? Does it build on what has happened before? Does it call for an appropriately ambitious next step? Is it feasible in the context of what is happening and what needs to happen? Does it spell out answers to the what, why, who, where, when, and how questions? You can also read and talk the assignment through with colleagues, staff, or consultants and get their reactions to the same questions. Ask them to play the role of the recipient and come back at you with the reactions and challenges the recipient is likely to have.

Closure

Close with a clear next step. Once the assignment has been conveyed, what happens next? Does the recipient just run off and do it? Do you want to see the work plan in a day or two? Do you want a progress report in a week or two? Is there to be a meeting to go over the strategy for responding to the assignment next week? Whatever you want, make it clear. You are not just casting a stone into a pond to make waves and then sink. You are starting a work process that must carry forward and close successfully. So be clear about what the next step is to be.

Written Assignments

The demand is reduced to writing in a clear written assignment. You can refer back to Chapter 2, Define Your Assignment—in Writing, for good examples.

The Psychology of Demand Making

Emotions are always in play when assignments are made. Both the demand maker and the recipient are moved at a very basic level by emotional reactions.

On the Demand Maker's Side

Someone who makes a demand always feels some concern about how the assignment will be received. Will the recipient be complimented by the opportunity to contribute? Will the recipient fully understand what is being asked? Will there be push-back? Will I have to pull back the assignment, or give ground on what I'm looking for, or on the target date? Will I be asked to give more help, more resources, more training, more tools—things I might or might not have? Do I feel guilty piling on more work for someone who already has plenty to do? Am I handing off a responsibility to someone else because I just don't know how to deal with it (but I should)?

Concerns like these can vitiate the demand. Yet when a demand is made it needs to be solid—not nonnegotiable, but well enough conceived that the recipient can understand that it is serious. Think through what you need to have done—and, perhaps more important, *feel* through it; if you're solidly convinced of the need to act, you can feel confident about holding your ground in the face of significant push-back. To help increase your own awareness of your demand-making patterns and how to improve them, work thorough the questionnaire at the end of this chapter. It covers the key aspects of the demand-response process for managers.

On the Recipient's Side

Your feelings can be very positive if the assignment is exciting. They can be negative if you are overwhelmed, confused, or insulted by the assignment. Sometimes people feel they have no choice but to accept an assignment as given, even though they have concerns. They "suck it up" and go ahead—but pay a price in terms of stress, fatigue, or worse if they persist in taking on assignments that are off target. Satisfying as instant obedience might be, you will be better off in the long run if you share your reactions and discuss the details of an assignment until it makes sense.

The Dynamics of Demand Making

If you are a solo manager with one subordinate, the dynamics of demand making are simple. It is a one-to-one transaction: you request, your subordinate complies or negotiates a response.

More likely, you have staff involved as well as your subordinate, and also peers and superiors to deal with. Instead of one-to-one, you are in a triangle of relationships—or a hexagon or more.

If staff is involved, then you have a triangle like the one shown in Figure 7-1. The basic dynamic involves the demand maker who conveys the demand and the assignment directly to the subordinate who is to be the project leader. The subordinate then calls on the staff to provide help. The staff provides support to the requesting project leader.

It's essential to be clear about the relative roles. Why is each a party to this demand? What is each to contribute? Are you looking to the staff to take the lead? Or are you looking to the subordinate line manager to take the lead, with the help of the staff? Are you asking the staff to work with both of you to provide data, insight, and assistance? Or just the recipient?

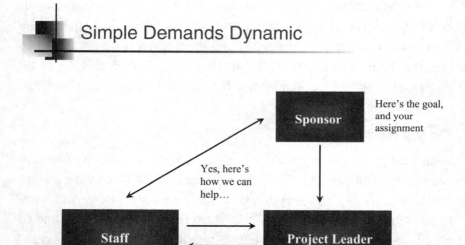

Simple Demands Dynamic

Sponsor

Here's the goal, and your assignment

Yes, here's how we can help…

Staff

Project Leader

Big job. Can you help?

© RHS&A 2003

Figure 7-1. Interacting with Staff and Subordinates

Things work best when the sponsor makes the demand directly to the line manager who is the project leader and who has the prime responsibility. This is spelled out in the assignment. The staff can then be of help to the recipient if the recipient wants that help.

Are you asking the staff to monitor progress for you? That can be a problem because it can put the staff into the position of spying for you, substituting for the direct reporting relationship that should exist between you and your subordinate.

If you communicate a sense of joint responsibility between the recipient and the staff, they might well succumb to confusion and work at cross-purposes.

It is also important to be clear about who has prime accountability—not just in the communication but also in the interaction. If a leader says one thing but acts in ways that seem to contradict that message, then trouble follows. If you make an assignment to one subordinate but then start having more discussions with the staff or with other people who work for or with the recipient, questions arise. When you ask someone to take responsibility for something, then you have to let them take that responsibility and let their energy flow. This letting-go is not easy for many hard-driving managers who might in fact know a lot, have tremendous energy, and want to be involved to make things happen. But they must let go if they are to multiply their impact and build the capability of their organization.

This does not imply that the sponsor does not monitor progress, nor get out and see what is happening where the action is. The point is that the follow-up should reinforce, not muddy, the essential responsibility of the prime project leader.

If other functions are involved, the situation becomes even more complex—like the hexagon shown in Figure 7-2.

In this kind of situation, make sure that all parties are aware of the assignment, have contributed to it, and understand their own roles and responsibilities. Make sure they all know who has prime responsibility for the end results and who is to take the initiative for managing the under-

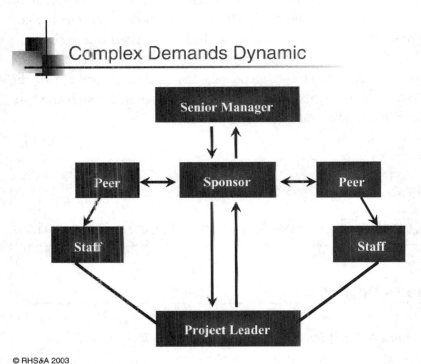

© RHS&A 2003

Figure 7-2. A Web of Relationships

taking. The written assignment is an excellent vehicle for making these issues explicit and working out the answers. An assignment memo helps bring clarity and consensus to the job to be done.

A Final Word on Demands

Well-thought-out demands mobilize effort and establish a sense of control of a work program. When you have thought through what needs to be done and have called on the right people to do what's needed in the right way, everyone involved comes away with an "up" feeling. The recipients have a clear sense of their responsibilities, tasks, and timetables for action. If assignments are shared and mutually understood among members of a management team, people have a greater sense of coordinated action toward a goal.

This feeling resembles the keen sense of urgency that makes people respond so well in the face of a crisis that threatens their lives or livelihood—a dynamic discussed in more detail in Chapter 13—which can be a tremendous source of power for effective execution. Good demands and assignments can have much the same electrifying effect as a crisis. A few good assignments that propel extraordinary action have extraordinary power if they deal with truly urgent and important issues, are keyed to the readiness of the organization, and have been thought through and conveyed with strength and finesse.

WORKSHEET

Questionnaire on Making Effective Demands

Selecting and Defining Goals

Expectations need to be clearly defined and focused. Accountability must be assigned. There should be a very few top priority goals. Note how often you make any of these errors:

	Never	Sometimes	Too Often
1. Establish too many goals.			
2. Define expectations in vague or unmeasurable terms.			
3. Change priorities frequently.			
4. Set target dates too far in the future.			
5. Fail to assign clear accountability for results.			
6. Don't check to make sure the recipient's view of the goal matches my view of the goal.			

Establishing Expectations

Getting people to fully commit to performance targets requires toughness, resiliency, faith, and perseverance. Do you see yourself doing any of the following?

	Never	Sometimes	Too Often
1. When my people insist that something can't be done, I ease the goals or give more time.			
2. I accept see-saw trades. ("Sure, boss, I can accomplish A, but you'll have to forget about B.")			
3. I accept reverse assignments. ("Sure, boss, I can get it			

	Never	Sometimes	Too Often
done if you'll get the other departments to. . . .")			
4. I accept vague agreement. ("Sure, boss, I'll give it a try.")			
5. I signal that the goal should be achieved "if possible" (rather than that it must be achieved).			
6. I hear myself offering inducements to get people to do what they should be doing anyhow.			
7. I permit offloading of accountability. ("Sure, boss, I'll tell Susie that you want this accomplished. She'll keep in touch with you.")			

Confirming Achievement

To make certain that your people accomplish goals, it is necessary to have work plans with a timetable and that you review progress regularly. Are there any weak links in your implementation chain?

	Never	Sometimes	Too Often
1. I don't insist on written work plans to state how people will achieve their goals.			
2. I do not review progress regularly—instead, I wait till we get near the deadline			

or when I hear something is going wrong.			
3. My people don't believe that success or failure will have significant consequences.			
4. I let my people get sidetracked on the preliminaries (studies, training, reorganizing, analyzing) rather than getting on with the task.			
5. My progress reviews are not detailed enough to spot the shortfalls.			
6. I do not forcefully confront people when projects go astray.			

Dealing with Reactions to Expectations

When people don't see how to deliver greater results, they might resist. You need to be sympathetic but also firm in your insistence that it be done. Do your feelings ever undermine your capacity to do this?

	Never	Sometimes	Too Often
1. I feel very uncomfortable asking people who feel stretched to do even more.			

	Never	Sometimes	Too Often
2. Unless I can actually see how a result can be accomplished, I hesitate to ask people to try it.			
3. I worry that tough demands will interfere with good relationships.			
4. I sometimes lose my temper when people resist—then I have to be apologetic.			
5. I worry that people will quit and go to a competitor.			
6. I feel guilty about my people working under pressure and so I do some of the work for them.			

Scoring

Rate each "sometimes" checks as a 1 and each "too often" as a 3. Then total your score.

>50   You're lucky. You have the potential of incredibly huge performance increases if you sharpen your demand-making skills.

25 to 50   You're not quite so lucky, but you've still got plenty of opportunity.

10 to 25   You've probably been getting most of what your people have to give—but perhaps you can find some room for improvement.

<10   Fill out the questionnaire again with someone who knows you *really* well looking over your shoulder.

Taking Action

From the items you checked, select the one or two changes on your part that could have the greatest impact on results. Make a note of them under the appropriate category:

A. Sharper selection and definition of goals and accountabilities.

_____

_____

_____

_____

_____

B. Firmer negotiation stance.

_____

_____

_____

C. Taking steps to ensure that goals are actually achieved.

_____

_____

_____

D. Overcoming doubts about asking for more.

_____

_____

_____

8

Follow Up Like Crazy without Driving People Crazy

Mobilizing an organization or a team to execute is a lot like getting a heavy hoop up and rolling. It's tough to get it started. It wobbles and twists at first. You have to keep pushing and pulling hard and fast to build momentum. But once it's got good momentum, you can keep it going with a light touch.

If you've been working along with the book, you've done the heavy lifting on your trial project—shaping the assignment, forming a core team, creating a strategy, testing the strategy while building a constituency, creating the launch event, building the work plans and controls, and making the necessary demands.

The next issue to address is how much effort and what kind of effort you need to keep things moving successfully. How light is a light touch that works?

Reject the extremes. The heavy-handed, control-obsessed leader is one extreme. The other is the laissez-faire leader who just lets people "do their thing." (See Figure 8-1.)

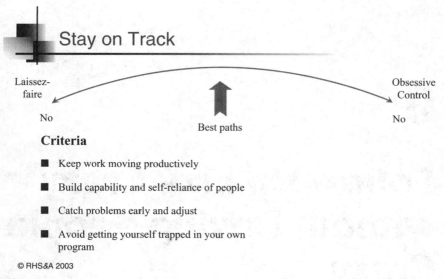

Stay on Track

Laissez-
faire

Obsessive
Control

No

Best paths

No

Criteria

■ Keep work moving productively

■ Build capability and self-reliance of people

■ Catch problems early and adjust

■ Avoid getting yourself trapped in your own
program

© RHS&A 2003

Figure 8-1. The Leadership Continuum

The obsessive, control-driven manager will delve into everything, call people day and night, jump into and out of meetings, perturb the flow of work—frustrated by the apparent nonperformance and quickly exhausting every scrap of personal energy and morale as well as the energy and morale of the team. Such managers might move people around, constantly searching for new people who will be "just perfect" but then become disillusioned when human limitations become apparent. Sometimes they will use staff or consultants to help. But if the help is used simply to reinforce the manager's unfortunate behavior, it will not be productive. If the help is used simply to do more of the work, the essential patterns will not change. If the manager wants help to change the patterns, there might be hope, unless deep-seated neurotic forces are at work, beyond the reach of typical staff or consultants.

The laissez-faire manager will hole up in the office and rationalize inaction. "It's up to my people. I've told them a hundred times they have to take more responsibility. I make the point by leaving them on their own." Such managers sometimes tend to rely on compensation incentives and performance appraisals to reinforce the impetus to do good work. But although these mechanisms have their place and their impact, they are also loaded with potentially negative effects. Financial incentives can become ends in themselves and drive effort off mission. Appraisals, unless very effectively done, can create more resentment and distraction than positive progress. Success is a very chancy matter with the laissez-fire manager. Neither of these extreme patterns are substitutes for the "right touch."

The right touch is the effective follow-up that reinforces and advances actual progress while it supports the growth of the people involved. The right touch differs for each group, each issue, each situation, and you find it through experimentation and testing. Effective leaders balance the technical realities of performance, the psychological tugs and pulls of involvement and learning, and the political pressures of "how it looks" to more remote but influential groups such as bosses, peers, customers, boards, unions, and regulators who make judgments based on appearance as well as on results.

Here are two examples of the dilemmas a manager can face in the course of this balancing act:

Andrew had put in a huge effort to establish an ongoing planning process in his newspaper operation, and he was sure it was worthwhile. Over the past two years, successive three-month plans and quarterly goal-setting sessions had proven productive. Productivity was improving. Quality was much better. Costs were coming down. Morale was better. And his direct reports were stepping up and taking greater responsibility for running their areas with much less prodding from Andrew and his staff.

But now Andrew felt at sea. He had resolved to abandon his weekly staff meetings and almost daily phone check-ins with his direct reports; the staff had been chafing at the intense follow-up that was Andrew's trademark. He agreed to switch to a monthly quick review, quarterly full-staff meetings, and possibly semi-annual goals meetings. With the general improvement in goal setting and planning, he hoped the new processes would carry the division forward with less of his personal follow-up.

After several days, he could stand it no longer and went for a tour of the operations to see how things were going. He saw people hard at work on the day-to-day job, but no evidence of work on the new three-month plan. He called one of his direct reports, who was away at an industry conference. He called another, who was tied up in meetings with the union steward to resolve a series of grievances. A third answered the phone and said the scheduled meetings to convey the new targets and plans had been delayed because several people were away on vacation. And some equipment problems meant contractors had been brought in for repairs and were taking the time of others in the group.

Andrew wondered if his program was beginning to come apart. He had never given ground on his management meetings before, and he was concerned that his change would be a setback for the disciplines he was trying to build in the organization.

But letting go isn't the only problem. It's just as easy to run into trouble on the other side:

Bruce was elated. A two-day conference had crystallized commitment to a long-sought organizational improvement program and set in motion several cross-functional projects to reduce costs across the company.

Four weeks later, Bruce reported in a telephone review with his boss that activity was under way on all fronts. New teams were being formed to tackle branch improvement efforts and work was on schedule. Experiments to test some new systems and processes were producing encouraging results. The cross-functional teams had held successful kick-off meetings. He personally was checking every day with his direct reports and project leaders. And his weekly staff meetings were covering the new projects as well as day-to-day matters. A major two-day review was scheduled two months out. Bruce felt confident that the operation would be on schedule. But the pressure of keeping up with it all was wearing. Bruce wondered if he had bitten off more than he could handle.

As these two cases illustrate, the manager has to consciously work out an appropriate follow-up process. The nature and frequency of progress reviews can vary considerably. It depends on the nature of the work to be done, the competence and energy of the managers running pieces of the program, how much change is being introduced, the leader's confidence in the organization, and the expectations of others outside the direct work program who have an interest in its outcome.

Review Strategies

You have a number of follow-up strategies to choose from, as shown in Figure 8-2.

Follow-Up Mechanisms

- One-on-one contact with team members
- Data reports
- Written reports of progress versus work plan
- Progress review meetings
- Site visits to get "outside" views

© RHS&A 2003

Figure 8-2. Review Strategies

One-to-One Reviews

The first option is to simply check in with people who are carrying out assignments individually, at key points along the way. How are things moving? What specifically is being accomplished? What issues are being encountered? What steps are planned to deal with the issues? What help is needed?

Group Progress Reviews

Getting the group together provides the most powerful review if it is properly managed because it assembles all the key parties in the same room and brings them all up to date at once. Begin by reviewing the overall goal and master plan. Then call on each of the subordinate managers or project leaders to report on their progress against their goals and plans. All can hear the progress. All can ask questions to clarify or raise issues or test the fit with their own efforts.

The staff report their views of progress on key variables according to their data, and thus verify or call into question reports from the line people. Issues are raised and debated, but then assigned for resolution offline if they are not quickly resolved.

These are the keys to making group progress reviews productive:

- *Brevity:* Each manager reports on plan and data, showing what has actually been done and the effect it has had. No need for long speeches or hype.

- *Candor:* Open, honest communication is essential. People have to feel free to be accurate, with no need to sugarcoat their reports. They have to feel free to point up problems or discrepancies. They have to feel free to raise issues. Bad news reported is good news. Bad news suppressed or disguised is fatal to a program.
- *Mutual support:* The mood needs to be one of urgency, movement, and helpfulness. The point is to help everyone be successful, reinforce good work, and deal with shortfalls in a constructive way.
- *Documentation:* Use bullet-point notes to summarize key actions to be taken and decisions made. Check off reported progress against the master plan and individual work plans, and update the data charts (introduced in Chapter 6). Then make sure that notes of all these points are distributed immediately. The notes start with the to-do lists as a ready reminder of what needs to happen next.
- *Integrity:* Integrity is crucial. Avoid the temptation to let progress reviews turn into whitewash sessions. If you're not careful to cut them off, hype and political agendas tend to creep in and drain energy into rivalries and put-downs.
- *Movement and fun:* The mood should be like that of a well-drilled team that loves its game. Such a team takes time out for strategizing. It huddles after each play to call the next. Progress reviews should have the same pace, spirit, and clearheaded honesty.

Progress review sessions have educational impact. People's understanding of the whole task improves as the issues are raised and discussed. But the sessions are not debating events or strategy meetings. Progress reviews are for progress reporting and planning of the immediate next steps.

Personal Site Visits

Many leaders make it a point to get out to customers regularly, and not just for sales meetings or golf outings designed to build relationships and to discuss future deals. They visit the frontline people, the warehouse workers, the purchasing agents, the technical folks. "How is my company coming across—on deliveries, on service, on product quality, and helpfulness?" They get beyond the numbers and the ad hoc crises that usually get brought to the attention of senior people. They want to tune in to the people with real-life experience of their company's day-to-day service. Then they come back and cross-check these perceptions with the (often rosier) views of their managers. And the debates get started about facing up to the realities of performance and dealing with the tougher issues of customers.

Sometimes managers create their own self-imposed barriers to this kind of follow-up:

> The commissioner of a municipal service agency had engineered a major turn-around in the performance and fiscal stability of her department. She had built a strong group of deputy commissioners and insisted they take full responsibility for their divisions. She studiously held back on getting into contact with people down the line, knowing full well that "but the commissioner said" gossip would permeate the halls and undermine the flow of communication between the deputies and their people and weaken their authority. When it became clear that some of the directors and supervisors down the line were not adequately stepping up to the leadership expected of them, and that some deputies were not really getting through adequately, she felt trapped. She had created her own barriers.
>
> After the next city election, a new commissioner came in. She had no inhibitions about getting out to the front lines and talking with social workers, supervisors, and directors to bring her messages about the need for better service directly to her people. Then she worked with her deputies to manage improvement. The concern about the gossip and weakening of the authority of deputies evaporated in the whirlwind of activity the new commissioner stirred up.

Special Reviews of Issues and Data

Even well-run programs run into rough spots. Some areas get behind schedule. Some wander into culs-de-sac and are stymied. Others head off in wayward directions. The performance and financial reports reveal issues to be addressed. These all require special attention. Problem-solving work sessions are called to probe into the issues and develop ways to get moving effectively.

Find the Right Path

While these are some of the mechanisms to follow up and keep programs and projects on track, making the adjustments in one's own leadership pattern is not so easy. It takes some work.

Andrew in the case at the beginning of this chapter had cut back his review process, but then he had to restore it.

Andrew got a reminder memo out to his people, pointing out that the progress review was coming up in three weeks, at which point he would expect to hear progress on the new three-month plan. He had no real contact with the program until then. It was not nearly as bad as he had feared; some good work was under way, but some of the progress reports were a little too glossy to believe and others were clearly off track.

Andrew didn't respond immediately. Instead, he called a special dinner meeting with his direct reports a week later and shared his views; all agreed that some of Andrew's follow-up and prodding still mattered and that they had jumped too far to cut back. They worked out a new reporting schedule.

Bruce, in the second case at the beginning of this chapter, felt everything was under control, but learned later that he was too buried in his project. Bruce continued to make good progress with his programs, but his bosses were concerned that he was not working well enough with his peers. They felt he wasn't pitching in adequately on new issues facing the company. He remained trapped in his program and was unable to break free enough to step up his contribution on other matters.

It is not easy to shift the way you go about following up, because you are changing basic behavior patterns. The process of testing and adjusting always involves some anxiety and struggle. What's right for you? Take a few minutes to assess your own follow-up processes on this chapter's worksheet. What's going well? What not so well? What shifts might be tested to get on a better path? What steps will you take to set these changes into motion? Talk with your people and trusted colleagues who might have some perspective that will also be helpful.

With a little thought such as this, you can develop better ways and see how they work. That is the essence of managing the follow-up process.

WORKSHEET:

Follow-up

1. What follow-up mechanisms are you using?

   _____

   _____

   _____

2. How is your project moving?

   _____

   _____

   _____

3. What's going well? Not so well?

   _____

   _____

   _____

4. What issues do you see ahead?

   _____

   _____

   _____

5. What adjustments will you make in your follow-up processes to improve?

   _____

   _____

   _____

Deal with Tough Issues

9

Use Political Skills to Win Constituents and Overcome Opposition

Political skill is essential to get things done in an organization. You made a start on this process when doing the reconnaissance to test your strategy, as outlined in Chapter 4. Then you uncovered issues to deal with, discovered the attitudes of people with respect to your strategy, and made adjustments to your strategy to accommodate what you learned. In this chapter, we get into greater depth on the politics of execution to deal with some of the more difficult issues. For great execution, five basic political skills are crucial:

- Focus on readiness rather than resistance.
- Get behind the masks that difficult people wear.
- Build a mission and a constituency that can win.
- Communicate a consistent message strategically.
- Deal with the unengageable few.

Focus on Readiness

The most important point is to focus on readiness, not resistance. *Readiness* is what people are willing and able to do, what they are motivated to do. Your job as manager is to enlist people and to engage them in the pursuit of a goal. Your basic approach should be to seek out readiness and then knit together the various strands of readiness in the organization to build and carry out a program. Knowing how to locate and tap readiness is the primary political skill of managers. This is easy enough with a big, challenging goal in front of everyone, when the demands for action are clear; it is harder but even more essential when the pressure is not so great.

When you focus on readiness, you will have less need to deal with obstruction, diversion, or opposition. Much of the resistance managers encounter is, believe it or not, self-created. If you are preoccupied with winning your point, pushing your program, besting a rival, or attracting attention in heroic fashion, you will probably be bypassing what people are ready to do—so they naturally push back. By contrast, even when change must be dramatic and fast and hard for people to accept, there is usually—if not always—a reservoir of readiness, perhaps buried and hard to see, upon which to build. Work hard to ferret it out, to cultivate it, and energize action accordingly. Once you take this perspective, you will usually find so much readiness that virtually all your time and energy will be consumed managing it for accomplishment of your goals. You won't have energy for the battles. You won't need it.

This does not imply that you must be a passive, accommodating manager who does only what others want to do. Far from it. You have a point of view, a job to do, a goal to reach, a mission to carry out. You work hard to make your case, bolstered by facts. You make sure people understand the case. You help people see their own self-interest served by their alliance with the job, goal, or mission. You see that people are given jobs that they can do well. You provide the tools and help they need. While doing all this, you resist the temptation and the impulse to cross the line into battle.

This search for readiness means that managerial action is quite different from legal or political action. Legal action starts with a dispute. The work is essentially adversarial. The lawyer is trained to make a case and then win it over opposition. Lawyers look for strong points in their case and weak points in the opponents' case. Their program is to put forward their strengths, exploit opponent weaknesses, and win. Politicians, too, tend to operate in adversarial terms. They put forward a program, win allies, and maneuver over and around opponents to win their point. They are proud of their record *fighting* for (you name it). Theirs is largely a win/lose game, even though they espouse collaboration.

Very good lawyers and very good politicians can do both—manage collaboration and manage adversarial action. Good managers can do both as well. But the really great managers, those who are truly adept at locating, tapping, and mobilizing readiness, spend nearly all their time evoking collaboration. When that is done well, resistance diminishes if not evaporates. Hard, constructive debate doesn't disappear, but battles erupt only when it becomes necessary to go beyond readiness, or the manager treads unnecessarily on areas of dispute and discomfort—or becomes frustrated and succumbs to the need to vent. Here's an example of effective readiness management:

Bernie H. was an Assistant Commissioner for Curriculum for Elementary and Secondary Education in his state. His assignment was to lead the "redesign of education"—one of the top three priorities of the department. Bernie mobilized a small team—20 or so people—to define a "new system" of education. It called for escape from the traditional teacher-student mode in which kids learned rote responses to tightly prescribed curricula defined by his agency. The aim was to focus instead on building learning processes by which students learned and gained skills and knowledge. It called for revolutionizing the structure of school districts wherein administrators and teachers ran things and parents and students were mere objects. The aim was to create community, parent, and student involvement in the design and execution of education.

After a year of hard conceptual work, the planning team managed to define and agree on the characteristics of the new system. Having agreement among 20 fervent advocates was good. But the state had 700 school districts, two million children, and a host of organized constituent groups: teachers, administrators, and unions for every segment of administration; legislators; school boards; regional service agencies and regional planning agencies; and hundreds of community action groups. Each had its own agenda, its own needs. None could have cared much about 20 bureaucrats who had an idea. Neither could the nearly

3000 other people in the State Education Department itself—those uninvolved in the redesign planning.

Some on the planning team were pessimistic. Contemplating the job ahead of them, they saw no way to succeed. But Bernie saw a way clear. Sure, there was enormous inertia and much potential opposition. But what about readiness? After all, even if the entire state were ready right now, how many districts did the people on the team think they could really cope with practically? Four, it turned out.

So why not find four districts that were interested and work with them? How many people from the department would they need to work with four districts? Forty. So the program moved into action, not by trying to transform resistant millions but by getting four districts to try something new, with 40 department of education people also ready to try something new to help them. That simple shift of focus—from struggling against all the resistance to tapping the immediate readiness—turned the trick.

Over the course of a year, four district efforts got off the ground. Within two years, reading scores were going up in the tough urban district. Dropout rates were declining in the rural district. The suburban district created a whole new kind of middle school program. So did the small city district. By the third year, regional planning agencies joined in. They mobilized more than 200 additional redesign districts to carry out their own experiment in moving to a new system of education. As the program got moving, the state department of education offered help from department people and small amounts of planning money to help districts organize their efforts.

The state helped reinforce readiness. But Bernie's original focus on readiness rather than resistance was the key for shifting from concept to execution. And it was a key tactic that he and his people used over and over again to keep the effort moving forward through many challenges. Almost any project can be addressed in the same fashion to build momentum and reduce resistance until it melts away in the face of success.

Get Behind the Masks

Still, you have to deal with real people—some of whom are sure to be resistant, obstructive, or actual opponents of your program. Or so it appears. The next skill is getting close enough to these people to find out what's going on behind the apparent indifference or resistance. Often it is a mask. Everyone is striving for something. They all have responsibilities and unique ways of relating to and working with others. You need to understand these factors when dealing with key people. Of course you see resistance when you put your interests up against theirs and they don't match. Well, whose problem is that? It's yours until you talk with them long enough to learn what they are trying to accomplish and what their vital interests are. Listen carefully, and you might well find unsuspected common ground. You might also find that you simply aren't trusted enough to get a hearing. So you need to grasp at any wisp of common interest and respond to it in a way that builds some trust and opens the way for further collaboration. For example:

Bernie entered the office of the superintendent of the urban school district taking part in the redesign. Although the district board had agreed to participate, the superintendent herself was very skeptical. "You state people have no idea what's going on here," she said. "You bring down your edicts, your rules, and then you leave. No help. No money. No idea what it takes do what you ask."

Bernie responded: "This is different. We in the State Department are going to deliver. We have to change too. What do you really need?"

"How about a typewriter? I don't even have one in the superintendent's office. And you want us to redesign education—ha!"

"I'll prove what I am saying about the Department," Bernie said, and left. The next day he picked up a typewriter from his office, drove back to the local district, and delivered it to the superintendent.

The superintendent, though still skeptical, was impressed enough with Bernie's intensity and responsiveness to agree to schedule a working meeting with her staff, Bernie, and the key state people to talk through what redesign might mean in the district and how they might start. Small step by small step, the collaboration grew. A year later, reading scores were soaring because community people, teachers, parents, and kids had all agreed to tackle that as a redesign goal that meant something to them, and the state people were helping.

The key is to find out what people need and tie it to what you need. It isn't always something simple and physical like a typewriter. For example:

Bernie had a similar problem working up in the State Department hierarchy. Despite top-level support, the official who controlled budgets and programs saw Bernie's people as starry-eyed theoreticians, and he wasn't impressed. He wanted to see concrete plans, budgets, schedules—the stuff that successful programs are made of—and he wouldn't move to help or find funding without good plans.

Hearing this out, Bernie realized that he wasn't really coping with an opponent—although that's what it looked and felt like. He took a deep breath and got together with his program team to work out a real program plan and budget with results targets, staffing lists, and schedules. This was cold, difficult stuff for people who were launching what was only an experiment that dealt with changes in relationships and concepts, more than bricks, books, and exams. But they created specific and tangible program elements, such as proposed timetables for implementation of specific pieces of work, staffing for the various tasks, measurements of impact. Bernie then got the support of the budget and program officer, and his financing as well.

Meshing different needs in this fashion is often the key to political and program success. In this case, the planning exercise also made the program more concrete. By going behind another mask of opposition and finding the vital interest and responding to it, Bernie not only defused resistance that could have stopped his program in its tracks, but also strengthened the program.

Build a Mission and a Constituency

You have a purpose in mind. Get it in writing, and use it for building a constituency. This is the third key political skill. Here's how it looks in action:

Another Bernard, CEO of an insurance company, sat down to draft a few carefully honed paragraphs about his vision for the company and major changes needed for success in the immediate future. The announcement would follow two years of intensive cost reduction and basic performance improvement that had been designed to get the company's cost platform at competitive levels.

His draft became a vehicle for head-to-head meetings with his top four lieutenants and a professor serving as a consultant. Every word was scrutinized. The underlying convictions of the executives were tested. The group gradually agreed that the company would narrow its focus to business insurance only. It would shift its underwriting radically. Having been willing to accept many risks that others would not, the company had become a favorite of brokers, but it was not nearly profitable enough. So the big break had to be made—dropping poor risks, upgrading underwriting standards, retraining all the underwriters and brokers.

Use Political Skills to Win Constituents

"We might be smaller, but we'll be more prosperous," Bernard said in dozens of meetings with managers and staff throughout the company. Through this dialogue about future direction of the business, the constituency supporting these ideas enlarged. The new strategies became the basis for the next wave of action.

Having a concept as a starting point, you can begin to reach out to engage people to work with you. Just as you did when testing your strategy (Chapter 4), start with a circle of people most closely allied with you, those most interested, those with the most to gain, those most ready and able to commit energy and help. Next, draw a second and third circle for those less ardent. Then get to the circles of people who will have negative or opposing positions. These are people who might have other aspirations that are counter to or competitive to yours. Or they might feel they have something to lose because of your effort. Or they might not want to be disturbed nor have their comfortable routines upset. The resulting diagram is a map of constituents—like the one illustrated in Figure 9-1—

Map the Players

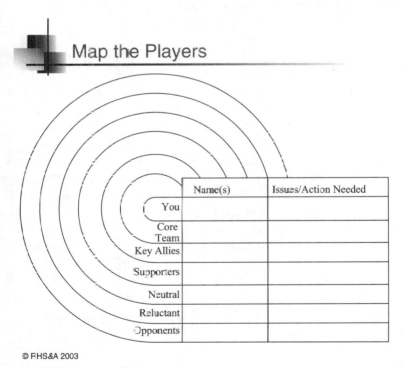

	Name(s)	Issues/Action Needed
You		
Core Team		
Key Allies		
Supporters		
Neutral		
Reluctant		
Opponents		

Figure 9-1. Map the Players

that can serve as the basis for interaction you'll need to have as you create your strategy and constituency.

Make notes of the kinds of issues you'll be dealing with in each of the several circles. Think about the strategies you can employ to win each interest group. Everyone will have substantive ideas and needs to be considered and built into the strategy. Some people will also want to be recognized explicitly. Some will extract a specific price for their participation. Others will require tougher responses to deal with their issues—formal negotiation, arbitration, or penalties, or separation strategies to minimize their negative impact.

Have your responses lined up. What are you willing to offer in the way of help, participation, and recognition? What are you willing to pay for specific needs that people might have? How far are you willing to go to compromise or modify the elements of your strategy? What would you want in return that others might be willing to give?

Here's how one leader changed the economic and political context in the organization to create a constituency for a new goal:

Ted was chief medical officer of a major specialty hospital in New York City. He was also chairman of the Department of Surgery—and thus in a very powerful position all told. Ted's mission, backed up by the Board of Trustees, was to enhance the quality of practice and efficiency of operation of the medical staff. He and the Board were convinced that this required moving doctors into full-time practice at the hospital. Having the full resources of laboratories and research close at hand, practitioners would be better able to keep up with rapid advances in their field. They would benefit from closer interchange among colleagues. They would participate far more intently in clinical rounds, conferences, and teaching activities, the heart of quality assurance in medicine.

Talking with his fellow service chiefs and other key doctors, he heard plenty of lip service supporting his views. But opposition was never far from the surface. People always hedged their remarks with a litany of disadvantages and risks. And none showed any inclination to actually make the move to close a private practice and come to the hospital. It was not hard to understand why. These were premier surgeons. They had multimillion-dollar practices. Their offices lined Fifth Avenue, Park Avenue, Madison Avenue on Manhattan's Upper East Side. The wealthiest patients and most interesting cases from New York and around the world came to them. Enormous status, prestige, and money were involved. It was hard to see how the theoretical virtues of hospital-based practice could compete.

Use Political Skills to Win Constituents

Ted did some homework. He did studies to calculate the long-term costs of building a first-class doctors' office building at the hospital site, with ample parking and support staff. He calculated what he could offer to pay surgeons. He also did some economic studies of private practice. He found that after deducting the rent, staff salaries, insurance, utilities, taxes, and other costs paid by the high-revenue practices, the final take-home pay was not far from what he could offer at the hospital. It was possible, he realized, to overcome the economic argument. He worked through these computations with the Board and with the hospital administration to verify the numbers and develop support. Yes, if he could get the doctors to come over, they would build the office building and provide the staffing and salaries and benefits.

Next, the matter of prestige had to be tackled. Here Ted reasoned that if he could get three or four of the very top surgeons to join him at the hospital, it would be a wake-up call to the whole staff. They might not all come over, but he would have broken the back of the prestige issue. So he set to work with one-on-one sessions with each of the top four surgeons. He made the case for quality of practice. He made the case for the future of medical practice and the institution on which they depended. Then he made the economic case. And then he invited them to be his core planning committee for the new office building and the development of the support services to make sure it was the world's best place to practice medicine.

Gradually the resistance softened and the great breakthrough—the lightning flash—struck when the top four surgeons signed up and the announcement was made in an assembly of the medical staff.

By adroitly shifting the political and economic terms of engagement in the organization, Ted was able to create the strategic and political foundation for accelerated execution. That enabled him to fulfill his mission.

Here's a case that illustrates more direct and preemptive action by a leader to set a new course.

A corporation was failing. After four straight years of dramatic losses, the company was on the verge of bankruptcy. There was plenty of blame to go around. Alan, newly promoted to the CEO job, decided that most of the businesses of the company would have to be sold or shut down, leaving just four that seemed strong enough to survive.

At a management meeting with nearly 30 top executives, Alan and his planner laid out the case for change. Only finger-pointing came back. No one was willing to take the first step. All blamed high corporate overhead (something in Alan's territory) and "other businesses" as the causes of difficulty.

Execution, Plain and Simple

Alan acted quickly. He invited seven people to join him for a second management meeting—the heads of the four viable businesses, his executive vice president, his strategic planner, and the chief counsel. He commissioned the planner and his EVP to begin a rapid sale and disposition program for the remaining businesses, while he took responsibility for corporate overhead reduction. Alan thus acted directly to overcome the political and psychological barriers to success of the management program, simply disengaging everyone who had reason to oppose it—a quite different approach from Ted's constructive engagement in the hospital. But it was the strategy that set the stage for accelerated execution and salvation of the company.

Managers at every level—from the frontline work group up through departments, divisions, business units, and sectors—face similar political challenges when they undertake a management challenge. At any level, leaders need a political as well as a technical and organizational strategy to create a mission—and a constituency to carry it out.

To document your work on the mission, state the vital goals, and list in a few short phrases or sentences what is to change: from what, to what. (See the worksheet at the end of this chapter for a useful format.)

To build your constituency, engage them in this process so that all the people you need are able to understand and articulate the same goals—with feeling. When you have a strategy, vital goals, and a crucial mass of support, you can move forward more confidently and boldly with execution. Your people cannot argue that "we don't know where we're going" or "we don't know what this will add up to" or maintain that their effort is not worthwhile.

To organize your constituency, create a structure to manage the effort. It can be relatively informal for simple goals, but make it more formal for significant efforts. You are the prime leader. You have your core team. Form a larger planning or review group. Form task teams to tackle the specific subgoals. Form an advisory team for the senior leaders to permit them to provide oversight and to have a forum for them to work out differences they might have about the program. A solid advisory team can strengthen the whole effort by providing coordinated direction to their own people and tangible help, and by reducing functional rivalry and resistance.

Building a solid and comprehensive structure, engaging all the people who can help—along with those who if unengaged can stop your effort—all this is part of making your effort politically unassailable. Obstructionists and opponents will be discouraged by the large and solid corps of people going with you. But you have to use the structure. It can't be a sham and it can't be neglected, so don't create or promise more structure than you will seriously manage. If your meetings are routine and dull, people will lose interest. The program will decay.

Communicate Clearly

You know what you are doing and where you are relative to your goal. Do your constituents know? Should they know? Communicate and keep communicating—up, down, and out in all directions—so that everyone understands what you're doing and what it means to them.

Of all the political skills, this is the one that takes the most continuing attention from day to day. It is important in itself for avoiding misunderstandings and wasted effort, and it is the medium through which you bring your other political skills to bear. You can't, for example, get behind a seeming opponent's mask if you can't communicate well enough to be heard and understood and to hear and grasp the response. Thus it is a vital issue deserving close attention.

Define the Communication Goals

Any communication program has two goals: to help people play their roles appropriately in support of your strategy and to prevent dysfunctional action by people who are uninformed or misinformed. In either case, the communication needs to provide what people need to know, when they need to know it. And it should be provided by the medium that is most effective for the receiver. Those are the basics.

Develop the Approach and Plan

First, make communication an inherent part of the action. That is, build good communication into each step—shaping the assignment, developing the core team and strategy, testing the strategy, and conducting the launch events, special planning work sessions, and progress reviews. Each step provides an opportunity to communicate the basic messages—what, who, when, where, why, and how—as appropriate to that step and the people involved. Providing a little background to cover these points sets the context for any specific information you present or request you make. Such communication helps convey a sense of continuity and order to what you are doing. It helps people keep the overall goal in mind too, which is helpful when complex planning issues, policy matters, and requests for action must be dealt with, and it is easy to lose sight of the ultimate purpose.

Second, special communication efforts are needed when larger audiences than the core team and key players are to be engaged or will be affected. Use your map of constituents for the communication strategy. This means defining specific objectives of the communication strategy, then defining who needs to know, what they need to know, when, and how best to reach each constituency. Table 9-1 shows the kind of grid that will be useful for this purpose. In the second column, "you" refers to the one preparing the table; "I" or "we" takes the point of view of the individual or organization that needs to know.

Make a quick sketch of an overall communication plan. You can break out what's needed over the next few months, and then get started. Once you get feedback on how effective the communication is, plan and carry out further cycles of communication, profiting from what you learn in the feedback.

If you have a larger-scale or longer-term program, you need a larger-scale and longer-term communication plan. The question of scheduling the communication events and providing appropriate media comes into play. Staff communications specialists can help a great deal here. Call upon such specialists from the start, as members of the core team, if communication is going to be a big part of the effort.

State the Message Simply

It's a natural impulse to communicate all the good things you are doing and all the good things that will happen. Whoa—take a minute to think about the receivers. What is their point of view? What do they need or want to know? What effect will it have on them? Is that the effect you want to have?

Table 9–1. Communications Grid

Who Needs to Know	What They Need to Know
Boss or convening authority	Do you understand the assignment?
	Have you started?
	Are you on track with schedule, goals, budget?
	Are issues arising that might affect other parts of the organization, policies, or resources needed?
	How will I be kept informed?
	Are unanticipated consequences coming up?
	Will I look good (or bad) because of this effort?
	Will it be successful? When?
Subordinates and employees	What is going on?
	How will it affect me? My job? My security? My pay? My future?
	Will I have to do something? What? When?
	Can I help in some way? How? When?
	Will I have to learn something? Do something different? What? When? How? Why?
	Will I be consulted? When? How?
Peer groups and functions	What is going on? Why?
	How will it affect me? My function? My future?
	Will I have to do something? What? When?
	Can I help in some way? How? When?
	Will I have to learn something? Do

Execution, Plain and Simple

Who Needs to Know	What They Need to Know
Peer groups and functions (continued)	something different? What? When? How? Will I be consulted? When? How?
Customers, suppliers, distributors, partners, other outside entities	What is going on? How will it affect me? My business? My future? Will I have to do something? What? When? Can I help in some way? How? When? Will I have to learn something? Do something different? What? When? How? Will I be consulted? When? How?
Staff specialists: quality, financial control or audit, human resources, planning, information technology, technical support, others	What is going on? Have you considered issues in my area or specialty? Have you called on me early enough? Will I have to do something? What? When? Can I help in some way? How? When? Will I have to learn something? Do something different? What? When? How? Will I be consulted? Will I be held responsible for errors or omissions you might make? When? How? What action will I take?
Regulators and government agencies	What is going on? Have you considered regulatory and legal issues adequately? Have you called on us early enough? Will we have to do something? What? When? Will we have to learn something? Do something different? What? When? How? Will we be held responsible for errors or omissions you might make? When? How? What action will we take?

Use Political Skills to Win Constituents

You need to develop something they will listen to—and then repeat it over and over.

Start with the payoff for them, addressing the interest they have at stake rather than your own. For example, an enthusiastic description of all the good technology you're installing will leave almost everyone glassy-eyed; they want to know if it solves a real problem or saves money for them. So start there, as that's what will develop some interest and willingness to learn more.

Cover next the effect or impact of your program on the receiver. What will they see or experience? When? What will they have to learn or do? Next, specify any action needed now, so that is clear.

Then get reactions—allow time to listen and absorb the feedback. Most of the value of your communication is in the feedback. Did the receiver get the message? Was the receiver properly affected by the message? Is the receiver ready to act appropriately as a result of the message? Did you learn something?

Benefits of Effective Communication

Many things go right when you use effective communication. First, obviously, more people will be with you. Good vibes will spread, easing the way for future steps in your effort. There is nothing like positive buzz in the company cafeteria to help a program along.

More important, you'll generate beneficial feedback. Possible problems, omissions, and oversights will be brought to your attention early, before they get too big or intractable to deal with. You'll be more likely to generate new ideas that can help speed progress or make it more effective or efficient. More people will be more willing contributors when their help is needed.

Pitfalls of Poor Communication

Likewise, many things will go wrong if communication is not effective. At a minimum, you will cause surprises. And surprises always lead to undesired responses, diversion of effort, delay, or extra work. Resentment builds, leading to passive resistance if not active obstruction. Confusion leads to error, off-target activity, rework, and other negative effects. And you *cause* these things to happen; the responsibility for effective communication is in the hands of the communicator. If the receiver doesn't understand, accept, and act properly on some issue, who else can be at fault? It's easy to blame the receiver, sometimes with some justification. But fundamentally it is the job of the originator to assure that the transmission is accurate, complete, and fully understood—and accepted and acted upon properly. That is an inherent part of effective execution.

Use Many Mechanisms of Communication

In this era of digitization, the speed and ease of communication is mind-boggling. And the channels are so abundant that they invite overwhelming amounts of communication. But people still have only two ears, two eyes, and one mind. And the mind has only so much real absorption capacity. So beware of the seduction of fast and massive communication mechanisms, the overloaded message boxes, crammed e-mail screens, cranky cell phones, pagers, and IM devices. And beware the limitations of one-way communication mechanisms. You need two-way communication, not voluminous one-way communication. And keep the old-fashioned methods in mind too: personal conversations, meetings, memos, reports, brochures, books, and advertisements. They all have their place. Make sure you have an "elevator speech" ready—a 30-second summary of what you are doing that you can offer in reply to anyone who asks, "What's happening?"

Communicate Every Day

To start, you can make effective communication an inherent part of your work program, not an extra. Build it into your planning sessions, launch events, follow-up reviews, and corrective action strategy sessions. This makes it real.

At the beginning of meetings or conversations, provide a brief review—the goal, the background, the current status—to set the stage for the specific point of the communication. This doesn't have to be voluminous or repetitive, but it is helpful in getting your listeners on the same wavelength, recalling essential facts easily forgotten, and providing context for the point to be made. Teachers are very good at this. Take a lesson from them. Make it a habit.

Be specific rather than grandiose. Minimize promises, and stress actual delivery. Avoid jargon unfamiliar to the listener. Avoid gratuitous pandering. People hear "You're so valuable" as "but we'll pay as little as we can;" "We need your input" as "but I hope I don't have to waste more time on meetings like this and responding to silly ideas and gripes"; "We'll involve you down the line, every step of the way" as "but don't get in my way; I have to move fast;" and "We'll take care of that; don't worry" as "I hope I forget that irritating nuisance of an idea." And set things up so you *never* have to say, "I apologize for being late [missing my deadline, or whatever]"—do it right, so you don't need to waste time apologizing.

Far too much communication is really designed to fend off active engagement, enlist sympathy, or ease anxiety. Better to link the action and the communication. It will be more real, take less time, and help move things along better.

Get Feedback and Use Feedback

It's not communication if the message doesn't get through. Written communications are difficult enough, but at least the message is available for review. Spoken communications are trickier, and it's worth taking the time to be sure the listener actually got the message. Ask for a recap or response, and listen carefully for missing points, distortions, or errors. It can take several iterations, so be patient. If the receiver is getting the message, don't repeat and dwell. Move on.

If you're requesting action, test to see if the receiver understood the request, accepted it, and is now committed to act realistically. Beware of the glib "I'll take care of it." If it's not clear what "it" is or what it takes to "take care of it," follow up. If you hear a slight hitch in the response, you probably have a problem; deal with it right there.

On the other side, if you're taking on a commitment, be sure you can do it. Make a note so you don't forget or shift the idea. Memory can play tricks, and the results are far from funny.

Close each conversation with an agreed-upon next step. Agree on a date and time for action, as timing can easily slide around too and undermine execution.

To assure that more formal communication efforts are coherent, clear, and consistent from your group, make the communication planning an explicit task. Talk through the communication strategy and plan. Define key points to be made. Rehearse the messages with your team or a good surrogate for your audience. At the end of a planning meeting, take time to work through the summary messages and how and to whom they will be communicated. It's a good device to pull together all the discussions, which helps you test how well people really understand what is being planned. You can correct misunderstandings. Summarize all this in notes and distribute them immediately after the meeting. Seem like a lot of work? It's nothing compared to the work of overcoming communication failures. To keep up with communication, memorize the principles in Figure 9-2.

Deal with the Unengageable

If you have done everything to build and win a constituency, and the program is moving with good success and momentum, you don't have to worry much about people who are dragging their feet, undermining the effort, or creating active opposition. They probably won't have the critical mass to be effective. Nonetheless, it's useful to have an armory of tactics you can use when difficult employees, peers, or superiors do become so difficult that something must be done.

Difficult Employees

Poor performers, distracters, underminers really cannot continue in your effort. First, be clear in your own mind about the specific deficiencies you are seeing, and make notes. Second, talk directly with the offending party to share your observations and work through reactions and possible corrective action. See if you can come up with a plan for improvement.

If you do reach an agreement, support the improvement. Track progress. If it doesn't work after a reasonable amount of time, then transfer or separation has to be carried out. Again, with specifics in mind, hold the next conversation and work out a transfer or separation plan and timetable. It's best to open up a path to something better for the person, or at least a

Use Political Skills to Win Constituents

Do

- Make effective communication an inherent part of your work program.
- At the beginning of meetings or one-on-one conversations, provide a brief, appropriate review—the goal, the background, the current status—to set the stage for specific point of communication.
- Be specific rather than grandiose.
- Minimize promising; focus on actual delivery.
- Get feedback; use feedback.
- Make notes of commitments so you neither forget nor distort the idea.
- For larger-scale communication, develop a formal communication program.

Don't

- Use gratuitous pandering.
- Use phrases and jargon unfamiliar to the listener.
- Communicate commitments you cannot really meet.
- Obfuscate, distort, pretend to know what you don't know.

Figure 9-2. Communication Do's and Don'ts

face-saving path. HR people and employment law specialists can help with these issues, bringing to bear a whole technology for managing employee changes and separations—some of which have legal implications. These are beyond the scope of this book. Be advised to get good advice.

Difficult Peers

You don't have hire-and-fire authority with your peers, so you need a different strategy. But it's not all that different. First, be clear about the specific difficulties—what happened, when, how, and how it affected success. Make notes. Depersonalize the issues—that is, outline the behavior or the issue in terms that do not place blame but rather point out the consequences. Verify your observations with others you trust, who are in a position to provide their own observations.

Next, sit down with the offending peer and see if mutual understanding and a corrective action plan can be created. This might take several discussions. And it might take a strong position on your part to make your case and insist on resolution. If that fails, then escalate. Talk with your boss, your mutual boss, and validate your position and develop a strategy for dealing with the person. This might lead to a dual conversation involving you, your boss (or both bosses), and the offending peer together, to talk over what has been going on and work out a better pattern. If that doesn't work over a reasonable period of time, and you can no longer accept the price in terms of time, energy, and goodwill consumed by the battle, you might have to move to separation strategies that culminate in the other person (or you yourself) changing the game, changing positions, or leaving the scene.

Many issues with peers can best be resolved at the beginning of an effort. The negative attitudes of peers might range from total indifference through passive resistance to active resistance and onward to outright opposition. Most often people will be willing to collaborate if the expectations are spelled out ahead of time. Sit down with the peer and the bosses involved to work out the assignments and the relative roles and responsibilities of peers to help with the assignment you are carrying. Have the bosses participate in joint progress reviews. Now you are not alone dealing with a peer who might have other demands and different issues to work on, but who must still actively help on your effort. The joint oversight management process might have to be sustained to keep things moving successfully, but it is usually quite effective.

Difficult Superiors

Sometimes we invest superiors with a "halo effect," imputing to them all kinds of power, wisdom, stubbornness, and other attributes that they might or might not really have. For the most part, in reality, those in positions of power are just very busy. They are preoccupied with all kinds of issues besides yours. They are used to giving orders and having people respond without much if any questions. Some don't like people coming in with their problems, or with new suggestions, or new demands. Some on the other hand are more open, do want to hear from subordinates, and do want to help. Don't make assumptions, step up, talk, and test the water to learn what your boss really wants. And work from there.

If you have tried to get behind the mask of your boss but found no common ground and no satisfactory path forward, then try other tactics. If you can, talk with peers of your boss and see if you can get some insight and perhaps some advice on how to proceed. If that is not fruitful enough, escalate further to your boss's boss, and see what can be gained there.

If you're going "around channels" like this in a strict hierarchical organization, then all of these tactics have their risks. And you might pay a price, if not immediately, then at some future point. Here again, your own attitude is crucial. Is the issue worthy of confrontation? Do the gains outweigh the risks? If you feel like you're on the warpath and spoiling for a fight, beware—no matter how righteous your case. You are better off with a mind-set of inquiry, seeking solutions to a joint problem, and enlisting people in resolving the issue.

If you are getting the run-around and nothing is really happening, despite all the reasonable things you are doing, then a more assertive approach is needed. Make your case on paper. Get the several relevant parties together. Insist that time and attention be given to the issue. Put forward ideas a step at a time so they can be absorbed. Beware of efforts at quick resolution by managers who want to appear smart but are not willing or able to get into the issue enough to make good decisions. Hold your ground. You might end up a hero if you are right—and if you want resolution instead of retribution.

Finally, benign neglect is a workable tactic for much of the noise one encounters. Let petty criticism, cynicism, occasional protests, and innuendo roll away like water off a duck's back. Keep focused on the job to be done and you will get it done.

10

Use Creative Problem Solving to Overcome Unforeseen Risks, Delays, and Obstacles

Despite extensive and excellent planning, obstacles and surprises will pop up. What does this mean? You will have to invent ways to get up, around, and over the obstacles.

This takes persistence and creative thinking. As a lead engineer once exclaimed, "I'll never accept 'it's impossible' again!" His product program had a technical problem that was much more difficult than he had expected. He simply could not accept another delay, even though his boss had said, "You just have to face facts. You can't repeal the laws of physics." He refused to give up, nevertheless, and finally late on a Friday afternoon, after nearly a full day of brainstorming and debate with his engineers, one proposed a new solution that had some promise. The team spent the weekend testing the idea, which proved workable enough that by the next Tuesday, he was able to report in his scheduled review with the division management team that he had a solution. This came after he had pushed until everyone's back was to the wall. He learned that "impossible" just might not be impossible, after all.

Why Do Problems Occur?

Technical issues crop up when you're pioneering new products and new processes. And economic and market calculations can go awry. But managerial issues are often at the heart of the trouble. As Nadim Matta and Ron Ashkenas point out in their 2003 *Harvard Business Review* article, "Why Good Projects Fail Anyway," project planners often underestimate or ignore two kinds of risks—"white space risk" and "integration risk." *White space risk* refers to the failure to identify some required activities in advance, leaving gaps in the project plan. *Integration risk* refers to the likelihood that some disparate activities might work well on their own but not come together at the end when they have to be integrated to produce the final result. This happens quite frequently, especially in long-term programs such as major system development efforts, organization development, and economic development programs that contemplate sustained work over months or years.

A solution proposed and tested by Matta and Ashkenas is to insert rapid-cycle "end result" projects along the way—the earlier the better—into the long-term program. Here's one example:

A multiyear program to increase agricultural productivity 30 percent for 120,000 farmers in Nicaragua was progressing, but both the Minister of Agriculture and the World Bank (which was funding the effort) were concerned about getting a real payback from the investment. To deal with these concerns, they formed work teams to tackle different rapid-cycle efforts to generate actual bottom-line payoff within three months. One team focused on increasing Grade A milk production from 600 to 1600 gallons per day in 120 days with 60 small and medium-sized milk producers. Another focused on increasing pig weight on 30 farms by 30 percent in 100 days. The immediate focus was on a specific, short-term, bottom-line payoff goal—more milk, bigger pigs—not all the preparatory work needed to build capability, such as improving technology, upgrading distribution systems, gearing up government infrastructure, and the like—the typical content of an economic development program.

These rapid-cycle projects were successful and demonstrated all the elements needed to produce payoff. So white space risk and integration risk were flushed out early. People saw in a few months just what was needed to generate payoff. Short-term, rapid-cycle projects also produce innovation and help anticipate and get past obstacles.

New Product, New Culture

Sometimes a whole program needs to be treated as one big innovation exercise.

A life insurance company brought in several new top-flight managers who aimed to change the company, get into high-tech products, and key into new groups of customers who wanted insurance and also to invest. When asked to be more specific about changes to be made—concrete changes that would exemplify the new culture, Gerry, the executive vice president, said, "We need to move faster to get new products out. But it's a battle. The old operational patterns are so deep that it's hard to change them."

He set up a work session with the four managers most concerned with new products—the head of the life products business, the head of IT, the chief actuary (who was the product designer), and himself—with a view to tackling one good candidate product. It took several weeks to arrange the meeting, with much jockeying of schedules.

The first meeting was in a conference room with three white boards, labeled "Today," "The Future," and "Getting Started." The session aimed to map the current approach to new products, sketch a proposed approach, and then outline ways to begin to test the new ideas. "Remember," Gerry began, "We have to deal with the people wedded to the old processes who always raise a huge fuss whenever we propose something new." The group realized the first thing they needed was to be clear about what they wanted to do differently. When a proposed change is vague, people have no choice but to raise questions and object.

Soon the boards were filling up. The old process was a typical sequential series of functional work steps to build a new product, with no one really in charge of driving a product through. Given the ins and outs, it usually took two to three years or more from start to finish, especially if many state approvals were needed. Many product ideas never made it.

Meanwhile, the candidate product had a real problem: A leading competitor was already coming to market with something very similar. The company had to have its version in place in a few months or it wouldn't be able to get an adequate market share. So there was a sense of urgency and a real need.

The group mapped a proposed new process that called for up-front involvement of the downstream people, simultaneous action on parallel work processes, and a central person to drive and coordinate work to meet an accelerated completion date. They called for a series of innovation projects along the way to overcome the toughest obstacles. The team got more excited as the design took shape.

First steps were assigned. In one of the most essential, the IT head and the chief actuary formed a team to lay out software specs at once—taking two weeks to get workable designs together. This in effect would be the first innovation project—no one had developed system specs that fast before. Meanwhile, Gerry and the business head would work together to select and commission a project leader—someone from the old school who had credibility and could help win the support of the rest of the organization. The energy was booming.

Two-and-a-half weeks later, 25 people gathered in the conference room with the three blank white boards. The business head took the lead. These were his people. But the mood was much colder. Crossed arms, furrowed brows, and cold silence all conveyed skepticism before anyone said a word.

The business head opened the meeting. "We're here to see if we can work out a way to get our new product done this fall. We need it to compete." Slowly, tentatively, people began to respond. They laid out the current process, with considerable debate about some of the steps, the sequence, and all the times "it didn't happen that way" drawn from past experience. For the new process the business head just sketched out the ideas from the previous session and asked for comment as he went along. The questions were not about the logic of the proposal, however, but about its acceptability in the organization. "The chairman will never permit this." "We've learned you have to take your time with these things." "There is no way we can develop system specs first; we don't know what the product is." The objections flew. The flak was everywhere.

Gerry spoke up. "I've talked to the president, the chairman, and the new product committee. They'll support this if you think the approach is workable. And I haven't heard anyone really object to the approach, just some logical questions we'll have to answer." Silence.

The IT head and chief actuary brought out a huge bound notebook, three inches thick. "Actually, we've had a team do the preliminary software specs over the past two weeks. Here it is." People gathered around amazed—it looked real. "Maybe these guys were really serious." The buzz was starting.

The business head spoke next, introducing the project leader and passing around a preliminary work plan that spelled out essential tasks for each function and the week when the work would be needed—on the assumption that the project could be done in nine months. People seemed to be nodding. The plan had many of the right jobs to be done, and the timetable, when broken down, didn't seem all that outlandish. Despite various reservations voiced by Legal, Marketing, and Training staff, the discussion began to shift from cold skepticism to the assessment of the specific work to be done, and what would be needed to be successful.

After the meeting, the top team of four reconvened. It had gone well enough. But they needed more enthusiasm if the project were to succeed. It was going to take more work to shape a good plan. The project also was beginning to look much larger than anticipated.

To get around the obstacles and generate additional momentum, special innovation projects had to be created. First, a special project was set up in the Legal Department to accelerate the arduous process of winning state approvals for the new product—something the lawyers said just couldn't be done quickly. State insurance departments have rules and procedures and no one is allowed to go around these. A full-day brainstorming session did come up with a different approach, however, which involved going for approvals in only five states and preparing submissions with day-to-day interaction with state personnel. These could generate the initial revenue to meet the first target. Other states could follow for further revenue growth.

Within three weeks, the new action plan got under way. A joint Legal, IT, and Marketing "approval team" visited each of the five targeted states. The team brought a computer and printer with them to make immediate changes in the documents needed to win approval. Informal discussions with state insurance people were not normal, but by making formal submissions and being on site to have immediate "informal" reviews, the team was able to get quick feedback from the state people and modify the submission. This meant the submission would be perfectly correct from the start and eliminate the months of recycling for corrections typically involved. This turned out to be feasible and successful.

A second special project was set up in Marketing. Again, a brainstorming team met to find a way to speed up the training of sales office staff and brokers. The team elected to try a half-day teleconference to reach out to all offices and key brokers simultaneously. No more visits. In four hours, the team would reach more than 400 sales agents, short-circuiting a training process that normally took months.

Week by week as the work effort took shape, momentum and commitment grew. At the end, more than 1200 people had been involved, not only in the home office but also in branches. By the ninth month, on target, the product was out in the field—generating $5 million in revenue its first month. The chairman toasted the success at a glittering celebration that brought together hundreds of the participants.

The project exemplified how short-term innovation successes—such as getting the original system specs done in two weeks, streamlining the state approval process, and shortening the training cycle—can become the modus operandi for a whole program.

Also, step by step, a new culture was coming to life. People were coming out of their silos and working together. There was greater speed of action and excitement in the organization, although IT people and some others who were under heavy pressure were exhausted. A new product keyed to a new market was in place. High-tech solutions were coming together for administration of the policy.

The new culture did not materialize by trying to change the culture. Going for a new *result* was the key. By tackling a specific goal with plenty of short-term wins and innovation to energize people, the project was a success—and the new culture was a natural by-product of that success.

Improvisation Is Part of Execution

Facing problems and coming up with improvisations to overcome them is not abnormal. It's all part of the game. The challenge is to build in ways to cultivate improvisation and innovation as part of the job. As the cases cited in this chapter suggest, it can be done by breaking big programs down into very short "results demonstration" projects. These flush out the elements apt to be missing from formal plans and generate experience that shows how to orchestrate all the ingredients needed for bottom-line success early in the effort.

A second approach is to treat an undertaking as an experimental effort in its entirety. From that standpoint, you never really have failures, only learning experiences. There are no problems—only "opportunities," as one famous manager has put it.

Improvisation Tools and Methods

Improvisation can be managed.

First, when confronting a cul de sac or problem, just stop and think. Is there another way to get what I want? A few minutes of thought will often produce a solution.

Use Creative Problem Solving

Second, if your own ideas aren't flowing, talk to others. Just explaining the issue to someone else and bouncing ideas back and forth often triggers plenty of good new ideas. If that is not enough. . . .

Third, try the tried-and-true brainstorming exchange where people toss out lots of ideas and nothing is discarded or criticized. The aim is to stimulate dozens of new ideas, which can be sorted afterward to select the truly practical ones with high potential. If that is not enough. . . .

Fourth, use some of the more sophisticated technologies when the problem is more difficult. Analytical tools for problem analysis and problem solving can help in the process. Some of these come from quality management technology and get into the very fine points of root-cause analysis, statistical analysis, systems analysis and simulation, design of experiments, reliability engineering, and the like. For example, Pareto charts track the frequency of occurrence of issues in a work process (Figure 10-1). Ishikawa

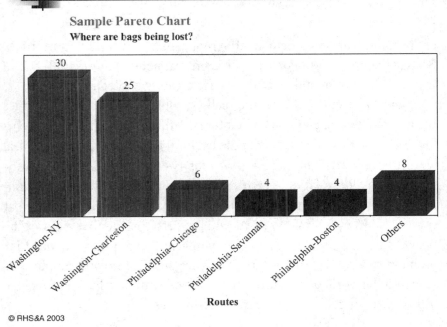

Figure 10-1. Sample Pareto Chart: Misplaced Luggage

Cause and Effect Diagram

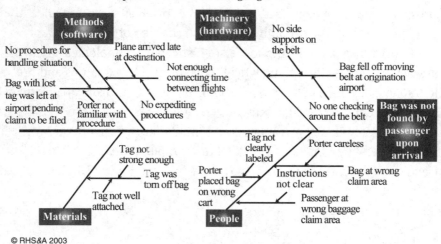

Figure 10-2. Sample Ishikawa Diagram: Lost Luggage

or "fishbone" diagrams help identify root causes of defects (Figure 10-2). Scatter diagrams help correlate different variables (Figure 10-3). All of these are important and helpful tools for creating strategies.

Many apparent problems are really "people problems" like the ones the insurance company staff encountered, rather than technical problems like the ones the lead engineer at the beginning of the chapter had to deal with. Improvisation on people problems is often a matter of empathy, engagement, stimulation, persuasion, and negotiation. Table 10-1 summarizes some typical improvisation issues, what's behind them, and what you can do to overcome them. As you get better at the first eight of the twelve steps outlined in this book, you'll probably find your need for problem-solving techniques grows less urgent. But no one should venture into the world of management execution without a backup supply of problem-solving and improvisation techniques.

Scatter Diagram

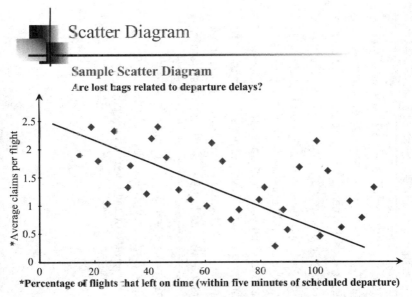

Sample Scatter Diagram

Are lost bags related to departure delays?

Data collected daily at one airport—see worksheet below

WORKSHEET

	average claims per flight	% flights on time
Day 1	0.25	75
Day 2	1.25	25
⋮	2.45	45
Day 30	1.23	98

© RHS&A 2003

Figure 10-3. Sample Scatter Diagram: Lost Luggage

Table 10-1. Improvisation in Action

The Problem	What's Going On	Corrective Action
People see new performance demands as personally threatening. They protest loudly and persistently.	The need for change in organizational performance has been translated into need for improvement in personal performance too hastily. People are being told that if they can't perform they will be replaced, as if that were the only choice.	Be sure to distinguish what "we" must accomplish from what "you" must accomplish. Many factors affect organizational performance far more massively than any issues of personal performance, so it is best to address the organizational side first. Enlist people in the common cause. Be creative in matching people and assignments so that you wind up asking people to do things they can do well. Give people a few chances to absorb and adjust to the new demands. Provide some help. Personal threats to jobs should be a last resort.
After an enthusiastic start on a project, people get anxious and discouraged. It's harder than they thought. They are missing their commitments.	A very common phenomenon. Most project teams go through "down" periods when they run into tough realities.	Hold firm; most people work through these periods successfully. A little improvisation, a little adjusting, and a lot of persistence will very likely pay off.

Suppliers (either internal or external) are late delivering.	People have probably over-promised out of optimism or the need to win you over.	Manage suppliers and the supply chain just as you would a project. When shaping relationships with suppliers, test the validity of their promises. Be skeptical. Get some early deliverables done on time to establish a pattern of successful delivery.
Technical problems are blocking progress and the solution is not obvious.	The basic facts of the situation might not be clear or might be in dispute. Or the assumptions underlying the design or process are not visible and the current situation is different from the assumptions in the design. And possibly the technology is just not working right and needs repair. It might be that technologies cannot interact with each other and new elements are needed to integrate them.	Gather the relevant data and test its accuracy. Get different points of view from several sources. Use charts and graphs to track data over time and get a sense of the direction of the data. Ask *why* and keep asking. After five repetitions, you'll unravel a lot of issues and get closer to the root cause—the basic issues to be addressed. Do root-cause analysis using fishbone (Ishikawa) diagrams to narrow down to the most likely causes of failure in a complex situation. Do experiments to test various hypotheses under different operating conditions and see what they tell you about what works, when, and how. Get expert help. But be sure the experts listen to you and then speak understandably to you. If the experts can't be clear, be skeptical.

Table 10-1. Improvisation in Action (Continued)

The Problem	What's Going On	Corrective Action
People say, "It can't be done."	Rules, procedures, habits, and traditions typically define what's doable. These can set false limits on what is *really* doable. You never know how real obstacles are until they are tested, and tested hard.	Be sure you really understand the rule, procedure, or whatever it is that is blocking you. Make sure it is not your misinterpretation that is the real problem. Understand the other point of view and then explore whether options are possible. Be careful—you're dealing with someone's emotional commitment to being "right," so don't threaten that image. But after identifying some options, and the reasons for trying them, see if a new path can be tried. Persistence pays—keep at it. People change their minds. And with some fresh and creative thinking, new paths can emerge. Don't accept "impossible" as set in concrete. It rarely is.

WORKSHEET:

Creative Problem Solving

What is the specific issue or problem? What factors are at work? (Describe as clearly as possible.)

_____

_____

_____

What is the frequency, severity, and impact of various factors affecting the problem?

(Use a Pareto chart, like the one in Figure 10-1.)

What factors seem likely to be root causes of the problem?

(Use an Ishikawa diagram like the one in Figure 10-2 to trace the symptoms back to their causes.)

Is project management a factor?

- ☐ Is responsibility accepted?
- ☐ Is the assignment clear?
- ☐ Do we have a core team and strategy?
- ☐ Do we test the strategy well enough?
- ☐ Was there a kick-off event?
- ☐ Are demands being made effectively?
- ☐ Do we have a problem-solving process?
- ☐ Is political management adequate?
- ☐ Have we learned from earlier projects?

What are possible solutions or corrective actions to address the root causes? (Get together with the core team and do some brainstorming.)

_____

_____

_____

Execution, Plain and Simple

What action will be taken?

_____

_____

_____

11

Energy Flagging? Manage an Intense Push to Get the Final Results and Rewards

In practice, people often lose interest in a project when their piece is done. Energy flags, especially if they've had some tough slogging to get through all the work. Initial novelty and excitement wear thin. And even people who are still interested might be called off to other tasks. So you might find yourself the only one left at the end who really cares about finishing and getting the total results. "We've done our part," people might say, implying, "It's up to you to pull it all together."

But it is your team's job as well as yours to see that the total results are achieved. So you have to do something to bring all the key people together to close out the job. It's not just a matter of inviting them to a boring final reporting meeting, or announcing weeks later that the product has been produced, or the sale concluded, or the targeted performance level reached. Such passive closing events have no zest; they make no visceral connection between the work and the results, and they don't reinforce anyone's connection to and responsibility for the total results. Instead, just as achieving solid execution starts with an exciting launch event, you want to cross the finish line with an exciting closing event. That will put a period to the current effort and set things up for the next one.

Plan the final event as a miniproject, asking, What is the goal? Who is the leader? What is the plan? Who has to do what by when? How will I get them all involved? Start the process by conceiving the final event itself—the goal or vision of what is to happen. For example:

- "We're meeting next week with the customer. We need the product samples and test results to prove it works so we can close the sale and get a check."
- "We have to present final results of our 14 productivity projects to the Executive Committee at a lunch meeting on September 1. They need to know what has been done so they can set targets for next year. Each team is to assemble and present its final results, summary project plan, test data, recommendations for sustaining the gains, what the Executive Committee should ask us to shoot for next, and the help we might need."

Announcing the close event is a call to action. And to execute, you need a leader and a core team, a work plan, a set of measurements, a launch process, and a review process for the event itself. Your overall project team members will scurry to button down the final results. Aides will rush to complete the final presentations. Staff experts will put the final touches on their supporting test data. Presentations will be rehearsed to be sure there are no holes, no open items, and no last-minute flaws—and any holes, open items, or flaws will be corrected.

Having to demonstrate a system or a product, or show a complete proposal to a customer or to senior executives or fellow employees or other constituents, creates powerful incentives to finish. Most people find it far too embarrassing to fail in front of a legitimate audience.

The final event can be an inherent part of the project itself, planned in advance and designed to ensure success. And it can be fun. Here are some examples:

Energy Flagging? Manage an Intense Push

A metal rolling plant faced up to the need to do better than its current 80-percent on-time delivery. Rather than trying to fix everything that might need fixing, it took on the goal of getting 100-percent on-time delivery for one trial week. The project leader (the manager of Manufacturing) kicked off several weeks of careful preparation with the Manufacturing, Sales, and Distribution people to get everything ready. As the trial week drew closer, he set up a daily progress review and planning meeting. He asked that sales orders be confirmed, raw materials be scheduled to be in place, and warehouse space and delivery trucks be lined up. The HR people put together plenty of hoopla to publicize the big event and focus attention on getting it done right—the first time. The team pulled it off. When the trial week came to a close and the final shipment left in time to arrive on schedule, cheers erupted—the workers felt like a baseball team that had won a perfect game. The trial week served as an extended "close event"—complete with banners flying. Of course, the team also learned through this experience exactly what it took to deliver 100 percent on time and complete. The steps needed for the final push were just the steps to be continued as regular operating procedure to maintain the 100-percent performance.

In the insurance company case described in Chapter 9, the final event for the project team was a half-day video training session for all brokers. In this case, all the sales offices and key brokers had to be invited and signed up for the training event held in the offices across the country. All the materials describing the product had to be finished and distributed. The information systems had to be working to run simulated orders. The actuaries had to be on hand to deal with questions about the policy. The claims people had to explain how they would handle the claims. Getting all this together was the "final assembly and test" event. A marketing manager was assigned to pull this together as well as to secure the videoconference service, reserve the home office lobby for the celebration, and order the food. He held planning and progress review sessions several times a week in the six weeks of preparation. The evening following the training event, he had a reception for home office people in their sparkling lobby. The chairman attended and toasted the team with champagne. A month later, when the revenues came in as hoped, the EVP held a less spectacular but nevertheless meaningful event in his own office.

A manufacturing company revolutionized its product design and manufacturing to meet the extraordinarily demanding specifications of a far eastern customer. The manufacturing manager led the effort. A tremendous amount of innovation, trial-and-error experimentation, and just plain hard work were needed over many months. This involved redesigning the product, transforming the manufacturing and test processes, and building new skills with the people involved. The whole project was geared to a clear goal: "We have to deliver 40 perfect items in a row. And be ready to ship the next 40 in a row off the final assembly immediately—perfect, just as they come off the line—to get the contract. The final production run will be October 1. We'll deliver to the customer that day." Many trial runs had been made. Every flaw was tracked down to a root cause and fundamental changes made so the flaw would never occur again. No patches were allowed. Dozens of tests had been done leading up to the target date. Performance was inching up to the perfection required. But the final push event riveted attention on really getting it right, exactly, in time for shipment. Pizza and beer were served for the whole team on the spot when the job was done. More rewards came later.

Managers at any level can use this technique. Here's one more example from a clerical floor:

Work-processing supervisors in a central clerical operations center planned to reach "5"—the top customer satisfaction score from their direct customer offices—every quarter. In the weeks preceding the customer survey, weekly meetings were held to go over transaction statistics, the inventories, and the quality statistics. Calls were made to the offices to ask what other services might be needed. Scoring was done by independent quality staff. And the feedback meetings were minicelebrations held in conference rooms on the floors. A little food and some small prizes made the reading of scores and explanation festive, whatever the numbers. But these events reinforced the importance of the goal and the direct connection of every person to the goal. No one was satisfied until "5s" were registered consistently quarter after quarter.

Figure 11-1 presents a summary of the things to keep in mind. The event is planned like any other meeting or piece of the plan. It is in a sense a project in itself. So you decide what will be done, who will do it, when and how.

Sharing the Rewards

Make sure all the recognition goes to people who know they deserve it and takes a form they will be glad to receive, because botched rewards can make it much harder to get anyone to help with execution in the future.

Reward sharing is a big subject, beyond the scope of this book. Nonetheless, a few basic points can't be ignored. People who have executed a project successfully deserve recognition for what they have done

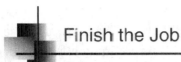

Finish the Job

Do's	Don'ts
▪ Plan an explicit closing event to bring together all the strands of activity needed to achieve the final goal and to get the payoff	▪ Leave the closing to chance
▪ Use that event also for sharing of recognition of accomplishment	▪ Distort execution with off-base or nongenuine recognition and rewards

© RHS&A 2003

Figure 11-1. Planning the Closing Event

and a share in the gains they have produced. That is axiomatic. Here are a few basic ground rules that seem to count most:

- *Simplicity:* People need to be able to understand the recognition quickly and easily.
- *Connection:* People need to see a direct relationship between the recognition and what has been accomplished.
- *Fairness:* People prefer recognition that is in balance with that accorded other projects, people, and organizations.
- *Justification:* People value recognition that they know they have truly earned more than a share of something only virtually or probabilistically earned.

I haven't mentioned incentives, compensation, or financial rewards up to this point, and for good reason. In 40 years of work with managers and organizations of all kinds in all kinds of situations, financial rewards were hardly ever the most crucial factor. Great progress was produced largely without special incentives and financial awards. That doesn't mean reward sharing hasn't been part of the game. It often has. But it is not as important an incentive as often assumed. Pumping in reward doesn't necessarily pump up results.

Financial incentives sometimes even interfere with excellent execution. So many variables can affect successful execution that shortfalls affecting incentive payouts can cause resentment. Arguments often rage about compensation when the underlying issue is actually fully success-ful, unarguable execution. So the time to distribute rewards is after the results are in. Baseball teams squabble over money in tough times, but they have little trouble dividing up the money after they have won the World Series. Sales commissions get paid when the service has been deliv-ered, the bill sent, and the payment collected—not just when an order has been called in. And when a company has a truly good year, it is a lot eas-ier to share the gains than when its results are poor or questionable.

In conclusion: Concentrate on getting the *results*. Then worry about dividing up the gains after they have actually been earned. You do want to have a formula agreed upon in advance, in writing, to assure people that a fair method is in place to share rewards, and to be sure no one tries to change the rules in the middle of the game or at the end. Life is sim-pler that way.

Two kinds of rewards are unassailable:

- *Actual Success:* People know when they have done a good job. And their colleagues know as well. There is an inner glow all around; nothing really needs to be said.
- *Recognition:* People like to hear those they value announce that they have done a good job. Nothing *needs* to be said to give people the glow of actual success, but saying something adds a glow of its own.

Perhaps the most effective recognition of contributions is an announcement made as part of the final event. A leader explicitly acknowledges the various contributions of the people involved. Recogni-tion of contributions by team members is genuine and it reinforces the values of teamwork and the skills of great execution. The mob of players at home plate greeting the heroic home run hitter in the last inning of a baseball game is one example. The pat on the back for the receiver of a tough forward pass in a football game is another. These illustrate the genuine, immediate, and clearly earned recognition of excellence by those who know what it means.

The world is full of other kinds of recognition: Prizes awarded to the "best" this or that at the annual meeting, Employee of the Month postings, award ceremonies for outstanding contributors, events honoring long-service employees. And of course there is the enormous array of financial rewards—as noted, a huge and complex subject in itself. These are all important, but their relevance for execution is less clear. Financial compensation certainly affects what businesses and people do. But few scientists set out just to win Nobel Prizes as a prime goal. Steven Spielberg almost certainly doesn't make movies just to win academy awards. Execution seems more a function of the ambition, energy, desire, know-how, and discipline of people to achieve.

WORKSHEET:

Planning the Final Push to Close the Project

Goal: What has to happen to demonstrate success of the project? When? How will success be measured?

_____

_____

_____

Leader and core team: Who will lead the closing event? Who will be on the core team? Who else has to support the effort?

_____

_____

_____

Plan: What specific steps will be taken? By whom? When?

_____

_____

_____

Measurement: How will the final results be measured? Against what criteria? Who will be in charge of testing and sign off of the results?

_____

Rewards: What reward and recognition is appropriate for this event? Who will secure them? What are the logistics of the final event? Who will arrange them?

Learn from Experience

12

Capture and Spread What You Learn

Take a deep breath. The close event is over and the results are in—but the project isn't finished. You will lose much of its ongoing value unless you invest some time in reflection and documentation designed to fix what has been learned in your memory and that of your organization.

If you race from the close of one project directly to the start of the next, or if you are in an organization that has a constant stream of projects under way at various stages and it's hard to know when one starts and another stops, you're probably missing out on the benefits of self-assessment and learning. Without self-assessment and learning, execution will not improve. Finding ways to generate real learning is vital to growth of capability, but it is hard work and too often avoided.

Generating Real Learning

The best way to learn and improve execution is to take a triple-barreled approach, combining both formal assessments with "in the moment" and "just-in-time" learning.

Formal Assessments

Formal assessments are conducted at the end of or at key junctures in an undertaking.

They are structured events with plenty of data and a sharply focused agenda.

The key points are these:

- All the key parties participate—the actual players, not just higher-ups concerned with the outcome.
- The group has a clear agenda and go-forward purpose to be served. The purpose of the meeting is not just to find fault.
- People arrive with a commitment to act on what is learned—and leave with the intention to take immediate action on the outcome of the meeting.
- A facilitator conducts the meeting to keep it on track and productive.
- Relevant data is brought to the table: original goals, actual results, key factors affecting performance.
- Everyone shares views of both causes of success and shortfalls, and key lessons and things to do better.
- The discussion aims to narrow down from the long list to the few ideas worthy of immediate action.
- The longer list of ideas is saved for further consideration.

The project leader calls the event and is responsible for implementation of the immediate action as well as future planning.

Here's an example:

A team of engineers building cellular phones for the far eastern markets gathers in a conference room in the United States for a formal "postmortem" of a new product project. Mechanical and electrical engineers and test engineers from U.S. operations sit down with test engineers from Japan, marketing representatives, and quality staff people who bring detailed charts showing defect, reliability, and cycle time data on every aspect of the product development process. The key issue is cycle time for a product set for the Japanese market. The product—a very small, lightweight device— has just been finished. But it must now pass customer field tests in the next four weeks. The schedule looks tough to meet. There has been a history of delays. The purpose of the postmortem is to appraise the causes of delay and see if new ideas can be applied to the next phase.

Capture and Spread What You Learn

Each engineering group reports its views of the reasons for delay. They each have a list of "do-differently" items—improvement ideas to propose.

It's not an easy discussion because in addition to all the objective observations, each group points to something another group has done to cause a delay. And this has created some contention. The quality staff people, acting as facilitators, work hard to keep the discussion objective. As they probe through the data with the groups, it becomes clear that the biggest delay seems to be between test engineering in the United States and test engineering in Japan. The basic product testing is done in the United States. The Japanese engineers test for workability of the product in the customer's systems and report back their findings to the U.S. project engineer and design engineers, who in turn involve U.S. test engineers—a process that has in the past consumed many weeks.

Can't the Japanese engineers be equipped to do all the testing? They plead their case for the full responsibility. But no one else is ready for that change. Besides, the Japanese contingent couldn't come up to speed fast enough to meet the immediate schedule. The group decides to send a few U.S. test engineers and some test equipment to Japan, plus one design engineer. This small team can work closely with the Japanese field test engineers to accelerate utilization of field test data in making design changes to meet the immediate needs of the customer field test. They all agree to meet weekly to implement the new processes and to drive the project to completion. They'll decide after the product is delivered whether the new arrangements really helped and should be made permanent.

In the Moment and Just-in-Time Learning

Less structured but also essential are "in the moment" and "just-in-time" training events injected throughout the execution cycle. "In the moment learning" becomes a habit—stepping back for a moment and taking stock of what is happening and what is being learned, and discussing what has been learned and how it can be used, right then, to move forward more efficiently and more effectively. This is valuable because it takes advantage of the "teaching moment"—that instant when people see a new insight and are ready to use it. You never know when a teaching moment might occur, so it's important to be on the watch and ready to exploit the moment with a small time-out for reflection, discussion, and action.

"Just-in-time" training is another dimension. Here, specific training events are held just when they are needed. For example, a project leader who gets an assignment to tackle a product cycle improvement project attends a personalized planning workshop the very next day to develop the strategy and initial action plan to respond to the assignment. An experienced engineer participates as well as a training professional who is schooled in the product development acceleration process.

Put It All Together

Putting these aspects together makes for a powerful learning process. Formal assessment leads to rigorous analysis and hard ideas that are validated with data. In the moment and just-in-time learning processes lead to absorption of new ideas, and changes in work processes and behavior patterns.

The overall learning process itself needs to be managed. It isn't automatic and it won't stick and be effective if it is not explicit and reinforced. After all, learning challenges habits and patterns that are comfortable. Resistance is inevitable. That is why so many organizations don't really learn adequately. A tough outside agent—a colleague, an internal staff person or consultant, or an external person or group—might be essential for this purpose, Someone is needed to push and support and make sure the learning happens.

The basic questions in the assessment are simple: Did we fully accomplish all that we set out to accomplish? What went well? What didn't go well? What should we do differently—immediately and going forward, to do better? The 12 steps of execution cited in this book can serve as a framework for analysis of the management aspects:

- Were the crucial goals clear and valid?
- Did the leader take responsibility and initiative appropriately?
- Did the leader have a clear assignment that was agreed upon up front?
- Did the leader form a good core team and develop a solid strategy?
- Was the strategy tested adequately with all relevant constituents?
- Was there an effective launch event?
- Were well-developed and appropriate plans, measurements, and controls established and used for the project?
- Was there an effective follow-up process?
- Were demands placed effectively?
- Was innovation adequate along the way?

- Were the politics and communication managed effectively through-out?
- Did the project finish off with a clear and effective final event?
- Was the learning captured and documented?

Learning events can go beyond just project reviews and deal with an overall management work program. The management team of a manufacturing company met for a two-day session to work on improving execution of their management program. These managers had done a great deal to improve the performance of their company over recent years through acquisitions, cost reductions, new products, and quality improvements, and were now underway on a number of new strategic growth projects. There was plenty of activity but too few results, in their view, from these new growth initiatives. Moreover, they wanted to move faster to achieve their immediate profit targets.

A small team put together an agenda for an ambitious two-day learning/work session for the management team. In the first hour of the session, the two top leaders called for focus on two crucial goals—first, making the next quarter's profit goals, and second, improving basic management processes to execute better on the growth program.

In the second two hours they made a list of their top-priority projects to produce next quarter's profit, and scored their confidence that these projects would actually achieve their bottom-line targets on time. This was revealing in itself. Some projects didn't really have bottom-line payoff targets; they were just lists of activities. Some didn't have clear target dates. Some didn't have clearly designated leaders. Very quickly the team saw clues to their implementation shortfalls.

In the afternoon, they agreed on how to manage execution of the immediate projects and to be sure that they added up to meet their profit target. On the morning of the second day, managers examined their own management processes for the longer-term growth program. What were they doing that impeded progress? What could they do better? A fascinating list emerged.

They were too busy. There had not been enough motivation behind the projects. They had not broken out short-term results targets before. There was considerable anxiety about letting go and really delegating some projects—fear of failure, fear of losing control. In other cases, there were no clear consequences for success or failure. In others there were too many layers involved and people were caught up in their silos, not integrating efforts. In some cases there was not enough teamwork—people wanted to work independently and not participate in a team effort. Some projects were very long term development efforts, but there were no short-term tests of feasibility.

They also discovered that they as individuals would have to shift their roles from being project leaders to being project sponsors and designate other people to be the active project leaders. And they would have to work as a leadership team to coordinate the growth campaign, rather than managing the projects as just more tasks on an already too long list of tasks.

In the afternoon they agreed on next steps. First, each division would have meetings with its managers to sharpen the immediate profit projects. In addition, they would designate the new growth project leaders and their assignments and lay out the review process for these projects. Second, the team scheduled time for their own progress review sessions to work further as a team to manage both the profit effort and growth program and help each other begin to make more of the needed changes in their work patterns.

This illustrates a way to construct a learning event for a management work program, rather than just a specific project. The event has two aspects: first, self-analysis and input on management execution processes; and second, work sessions to immediately apply the lessons in action.

Managers at every level can profit from processes such as these. When organizational peers meet regularly to review results and share ideas on what works, how to do things better, and how they can each lead their own groups more effectively, they all profit.

The 12 steps of execution can be used for part of this self-assessment so that participants can look at the full range of issues of execution. Figure 12-1 has a diagram to summarize the 12 steps. You can use the work sheets after Figure 12-1 to plan a learning assessment event and to score yourself and create your own execution performance profile.

When these learning processes are embedded in an organization's overall drive for better performance—and the organization is constantly striving for further significant gain—then the learning happens and is translated into better results, and better execution.

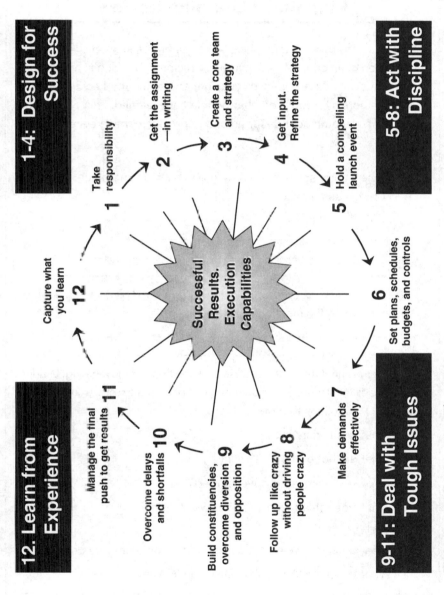

1-4: Design for Success

Take responsibility **1**

Get the assignment —in writing **2**

Create a core team and strategy **3**

Get input. Refine the strategy **4**

5-8: Act with Discipline

Hold a compelling launch event **5**

Set plans, schedules, budgets, and controls **6**

9-11: Deal with Tough Issues

Make demands effectively **7**

Follow up like crazy without driving people crazy **8**

Build constituencies, overcome diversion **9** and opposition

Overcome delays and shortfalls **10**

Manage the final push to get results **11**

12. Learn from Experience

Capture what you learn **12**

Successful Results. Execution Capabilities

Figure 12-1. Key Learning Elements

145

WORKSHEET:

Planning a Learning Review

Note: Learning reviews take place at key junctures in an effort, or upon completion of an effort. All key players participate, bringing in actual performance data. It's an open discussion, and someone keeps detailed notes so there's a record of what people have learned. This worksheet provides a skeleton agenda for an end of project learning event.

AGENDA

1. Review purposes of the review. (Keep brief, but make sure everyone is on the same page.)

   Original goals: _____

   _____

   Initial plans: _____

   _____

2. Actual results as compared to original goals and plans, and the gaps, focusing on the most crucial elements.

   _____

   _____

3. Discussion: (This open discussion is the heart of the meeting. Leader or facilitator notes items on newsprint or computer projector for all to see.) Questions to cover:

   What went well? Why?

   What did not go so well? Why?

   What key lessons have we learned?

   What does this mean for what we do differently right now? Top three to five items?

   What does this mean that we should do differently longer term?

   What action shall we take? By whom? When?

WORKSHEET:

Assessing Execution Success
for Any Project or Initiative

Factor	Exceeded	On Target	Fell Short	Comments. What happened? Why?
Were the end result goals achieved?				
On time?				
On Budget?				

How well was the effort managed? Assess the 12 steps to achieving any goal on time and on budget.

Step	Excellent	Good	Weak	Comments. What happened? Why?
DESIGN FOR SUCCESS Did the leader take responsibility and initiative?				
Did the leader have a clear assignment that was				

WORKSHEET: (*Continued*)

Step	Excellent	Good	Weak	Comments. What happened? Why
agreed upon up front? Were the goals clear and valid?				
Did the leader form a good core team and develop a solid strategy?				
Was the strategy tested adequately with all relevant constituents and revised?				
EXECUTE WITH DISCIPLINE Was there an effective launch event?				
Were well-developed and appropriate plans, measurements, and controls established and used?				
Was there an effective				

Take Responsibility–Who, Me?

follow-up process?				
DEAL WITH TOUGH ISSUES Were demands placed effectively?				
Were problem solving and innovation adequate along the way?				
Were the politics and communication effectively managed throughout the effort?				
Did the project finish with an effective final event?				
LEARN FROM EXPERIENCE Was the learning captured and documented?				

What other factors affected success?

_____

_____

_____

Execution, Plain and Simple

All in all, what were the main weak spots?

_____

_____

_____

What will be done to improve the weak spots?

_____

_____

_____

PART II

Accelerated Execution: Using Small Breakthrough Projects to Achieve Large Strategic Goals

Part I outlined the very basic elements of execution. As you get these under your belt, and your organization is moving better, you can start to accelerate the progress. Part II outlines ways to mobilize your organization to get moving faster and better. It starts with exploration of "zest factors" to tap the hidden potential already available. Then it describes execution breakthrough projects. These generate new results, momentum, and capability quickly. You can then build on the initial breakthroughs, step by step, to achieve larger and more ambitious strategic goals faster. You'll be on the no-cost path to higher performance and more successful change. Part II concludes with the key task of senior management—focusing the organization on the few most crucial goals that best drive big gains and excellent execution.

13

The Zest Factors: What Crises Can Teach Us about Accelerated Execution

Just think how much more organizations produce in a crisis than under normal conditions. Crises reveal for an instant the extraordinary execution capability of an organization—energy, motivation, ingenuity—capability not visible before. People rally round and do whatever it takes to deal with the situation. And nothing has changed except the urgency and importance of the challenge to be met and the level of execution to respond.

> The roof of a South Carolina carpet mill collapsed in a snowstorm. Only one of its three tufting machines was operable. Nonetheless, the mill still shipped every order in its book in the following days.

> An oil refinery suffering a strike operated successfully with one-seventh its normal complement. The evaporation of the workforce took place in one week as the strike unfolded and people left their jobs, but the refinery was not shut down. With no investment in new processes, new equipment, new training, or the like,

the remaining managers and engineers ran the facility—demonstrating seven times the usual organizational productivity. This surge in productivity lasted four months.

Extraordinary challenges provoke extraordinary responses. Everyone has seen them. The discrepancy between the output in a crisis and normal work output is enormous. These experiences offer some clues to the opportunity for gain through better execution.

The Triggers of Extraordinary Execution: Zest Factors

Why do crises produce extraordinary performance?

- The challenge is dramatic and visible.
- The goal is both specific and urgent.
- The situation clearly requires direct and instant action.
- The consequences are unavoidable and failure is unacceptable.
- The drama of the crisis stirs deep-seated emotions and commitment.
- Bureaucratic procedures and nonessential tasks are cast aside.
- Teamwork and cooperative action emerge despite old boundaries, traditions, and even enmities.
- Innovations and new leaders spring up out of necessity.
- Focus on the goal is unwavering, and action is not deflected by distractions.

Why Doesn't Crisis Performance Become the Norm?

When the crisis passes, performance typically drops back to former levels. This is not due so much to exhaustion—although human endurance has its limits—as to the relaxation of the very ingredients that evoked the performance in the first place, the "zest factors." Goals proliferate and become fuzzy. Urgency dissipates. Drama diminishes as humdrum routine returns. Consequences are unclear or avoidable. Well-worn but unproductive routines and patterns of behavior reassert themselves. These patterns conspire to keep performance well below what is possible.

Efforts to improve performance in normal times often do too little to inject zest. The programs involve analysis, process redesign, installation of measurement systems, and injections of wisdom, technology, or support devices of one sort or another. The results often do not turn out as hoped. The price paid for the gains that are achieved might be too high. Even costly motivation and recognition systems might fail to energize the organization adequately.

By contrast, great managers seem to understand the phenomenon of zest and use it to advantage. For them, the management job is not to exhort action, proclaim edicts, or just introduce new programs or techniques. It is instead to mobilize people to tackle tough business challenges with small, short-term projects keyed to longer-term strategies—that is, by creating in essence the planned equivalents of minicrisis events.

CNA, a property and casualty insurance company, saved hundreds of millions in operating costs by calling on each business unit to commit to a best-in-class expense ratio, define at least five short-term projects to get there, and execute and report on results of the first project at the next quarterly business review. The first projects were promising. And the managers persisted. They far exceeded their goal in a sustained effort over two years.

Management researchers and writers reinforce these observations and take them a step further. They are focusing with growing intensity on execution as a vital foundation for sustained excellence.

Larry Bossidy saw plenty of opportunity when he first arrived as CEO of AlliedSignal after his long experience at GE. He dove in with his considerable energy and great management talent to change AlliedSignal for the better. He reports that in his eight-year tenure there, margins tripled to 15 percent and return on equity grew from just over 10 percent to 28 percent. "How did we do it? We created a discipline of execution," he explains (Bossidy and Charan, 2002, p. 3).

James Collins (2001) distills more than 15,000 hours of highly refined research into what gives an organization a sustainable edge over its competition. He concludes that disciplined people, disciplined thought, and disciplined action are what determine who will make the climb from good to great performance. He found no heroics, no clearly discernible "great breakthroughs" nor charismatic leaders that consistently accounted for the gain. It was, he asserts, the steady, unrelenting application of his key points—the cumulative impact of small and mutually reinforcing advances that, like a flywheel accelerating in almost imperceptible increments, become an unstoppable force.

Nitin Nohria, Bruce Robertson, and Bruce Joyce (2003) studied performance of 160 companies over a 10-year period and found that strategy, execution and culture were the most vital ingredients for sustained business success. Structure was a fourth key element.

Exemplary celebrity managers—Jack Welch, Andy Grove, Rudy Giuliani, and Louis Gerstner, among hundreds more, have shared their views on what it took to make their organizations succeed and how they carried out their complicated and difficult missions—that is, how they executed. They offer plenty of advice for managers along the way, all of which reinforce powerful and sustained execution as key to their success.

It should be obvious. But as with so many other obvious matters that escape notice, how do you see through the fog? What can be done to make the issue and the opportunity dramatically clear?

I'll suggest a way not only to make it clear but to put a number on it that is right for your organization. You can estimate the potential for gain in your own organization from better execution. It takes little more than an hour to get a good first look at the size of the opportunity.

Estimate the Potential for Gain in Your Organization

First, assemble your people in a room. Turn off the pagers, cell phones, Instant Messaging devices, PDAs, and computers. Lock them up. Put them outside, far out of reach. All you want in the room are the people, undistracted people.

Second, ask the group to tell you about examples they have seen of extraordinary performance in a crisis. You can give them some examples to get the ball rolling, such as the carpet plant and the others I mentioned earlier. Show them a chart like the one in Figure 13-1. It won't take long. You'll have half a dozen good examples in minutes. I know, I know, you'll hear an outcry: "You can't expect us to operate in crisis mode all the time. We're already running around in a crisis half the time now." But you

The Zest Factors

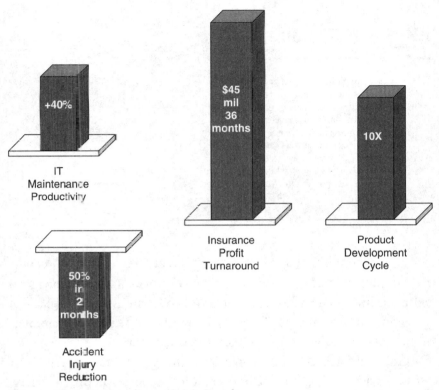

Figure 13-1. Extraordinary Crisis Results

can assure them that you're not suggesting crises as models of management, you're just trying to understand how much organizations can really produce when they have to.

Third, ask them to list what is happening in a crisis that generates the extraordinary performance. Rarely do people need much prompting to get up a good list. You'll soon see the zest factors, such as those listed in Figure 13-2 and more besides.

Fourth, ask them to list barriers to high performance they've seen in their organization. Barriers can be psychological—such as denial, finger-pointing, and patterns of victimhood—or they can derive from a need for more resources, more skills, better leaders, better technology, and the like. Barriers can also be organizational— poor communications, outmoded routines and procedures, excessive layers of approval, rivalries

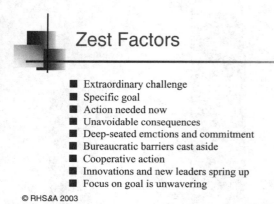

Zest Factors

- Extraordinary challenge
- Specific goal
- Action needed now
- Unavoidable consequences
- Deep-seated emotions and commitment
- Bureaucratic barriers cast aside
- Cooperative action
- Innovations and new leaders spring up
- Focus on goal is unwavering

© RHS&A 2003

Figure 13-2. The Zest Factors

among units contending for scarce resources and recognition. And barriers can involve management performance—inadequate strategy, slipshod planning, unclear goals, indecisive decision making, and lack of meaningful measurements. Take a few minutes to list some examples. The summaries in Figure 13-3 illustrate typical barriers.

Fifth, step back and ask people to estimate how much more your team could accomplish if these barriers were reduced and the electricity of crisislike events were injected into the organization. If people are reluctant to respond, ask them to vote anonymously. You can suggest three ranges like the ones in Figure 13-4 to make it easier: under 10 percent, 11–30 percent, 31–60 percent, and more than 60 percent. Average out the votes. Now you have a number!

My colleagues and I have asked these questions of thousands of managers. They never fail to identify crisis examples. They never fail to list the elements that produce the performance—the zest factors. Their estimates of potential gain often range from 30 percent to 60 percent. And many go even further, estimating 100 percent and more potential for gain. Reassure people that you're not going to cut their budgets by up to 60 percent tomorrow. Again, you're just trying to see how much is at stake.

Real-life experiences sometimes demonstrate even greater gains, however.

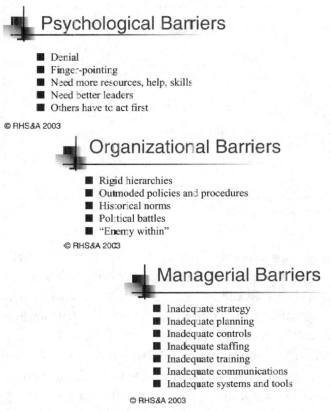

Psychological Barriers

- Denial
- Finger-pointing
- Need more resources, help, skills
- Need better leaders
- Others have to act first

© RHS&A 2003

Organizational Barriers

- Rigid hierarchies
- Outmoded policies and procedures
- Historical norms
- Political battles
- "Enemy within"

© RHS&A 2003

Managerial Barriers

- Inadequate strategy
- Inadequate planning
- Inadequate controls
- Inadequate staffing
- Inadequate training
- Inadequate communications
- Inadequate systems and tools

© RHS&A 2003

Figure 13-3. Barriers to High Performance

A PPG paint manufacturing unit got out a special order over one weekend—instead of the normal three- to four-week cycle for special orders—because its people saw a unique opportunity to win a new customer. This was a solid ten times their usual performance.

A Citigroup investment banking group, despite crashing stock markets, tripled its revenue and profit with a series of hundred-day accelerated execution projects that continued over two years.

Remember, the gains produced in these situations were achieved by the same group of people who'd been producing the former routine results, and they were using the skills, equipment, facilities, business models, and tools they had on hand or readily available. The only differ-

How much more might your organization produce?

	Your Vote
<10%	
11%–30%	
31%–60%	
>60%	

Figure 13-4. Room for Improvement

ences were the level of expectation and the level of execution. It's worth saying again: The *only* differences were in the level of expectation and in the level of execution. Now you can see the size of the opportunity—in general and for your company or group in particular—for bottom-line gain from accelerated execution.

I am not advocating that you go out and stir up a dire crisis nor that organizations should operate in crisis mode all the time. Extraordinary execution performance develops, step by step, by generating zest factors, using the disciplines of execution, setting gradually higher demands, and employing all the problem-solving and political skills that make work more engaging and successful. How can this be done? How far can you go? That's what the rest of this book is about.

14

Small-Scale "Breakthrough Projects:" Get Crucial Results Fast, Generate Momentum, and Build New Organizational Capabilities

You can build extraordinary execution in workable stages. The heart of the matter is the "breakthrough project:" a small-scale effort aimed at achieving a specific and concrete goal that is urgent, important, and that people are ready to do. This kind of project, as Robert Schaffer explains in *The Breakthrough Strategy* (1988), taps hidden potential in the organization and translates it into payoff. It replicates the experience of a crisis in its urgency, drama, and novelty. It serves as a prototype for great execution and a model for how the organization can and should work.

Execution, Plain and Simple

A breakthrough project is short term—usually 30, 60, 100 days in duration. It produces a bottom-line result exactly as intended—not recommendations, nor just a plan. It challenges people to move beyond their comfort zone. It is not just an activity, nor is it a good try—only a genuine success counts as a breakthrough. It uses resources readily available. It opens the way to further progress. It provides learning for all involved because it requires the use of the disciplines of execution. Thus it is the basic building block of execution capability.

A breakthrough project derives from a strategically crucial goal, so it is not just an ad hoc effort. The goal is defined by funneling down from the broad goal to successively narrower objectives and then to the very specific, quantified breakthrough goal with a specific date for achievement. For example: Increase profitability earned by branch offices/Accelerate the close cycle in fourth quarter, not letting sales slide into next year/Get 20 percent more sales closed in fourth quarter this year in the Milwaukee office. Figures 14-1, 14-2, and 14-3 show examples.

The three figures illustrate how breakthrough goals are stepping stones on the path to the larger goals—not markers or milestones, but actual production of output that contributes to a larger goal. To make them work, you have to stick to them—no giving ground on the goal once you're en route. Insist on success as it was originally conceived. That's what will make people face up to all the psychological and organizational barriers that typically undermine or derail execution. And that's the point: The aim is to build the habit of overcoming these barriers and actually achieving targeted results, on time, on budget, on spec, over and over again.

To assure that the breakthrough project is the vehicle for building execution capability, it's essential to distinguish between an execution breakthrough that builds capability and just doing something fast. Doing something fast is getting a task done today, not tomorrow. It is getting a quick win or plucking low-hanging fruit: an easy accomplishment. There is nothing wrong with doing something fast, nor with getting a quick win to gather low-hanging fruit. But that is all you get when you do something fast simply because it can be done fast. There is no breaking out of self-limiting patterns of management, no new experience using the disciplines of execution, no opening up of new possibilities.

Small-Scale "Breakthrough Projects"

Example

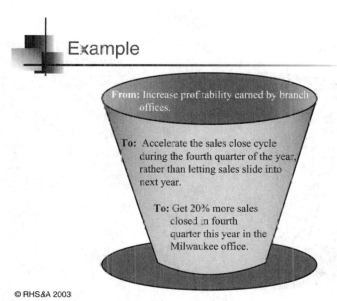

From: Increase profitability earned by branch offices.

To: Accelerate the sales close cycle during the fourth quarter of the year, rather than letting sales slide into next year.

To: Get 20% more sales closed in fourth quarter this year in the Milwaukee office.

© RHS&A 2003

Figure 14-1. Breakthrough: Sales Target

Example

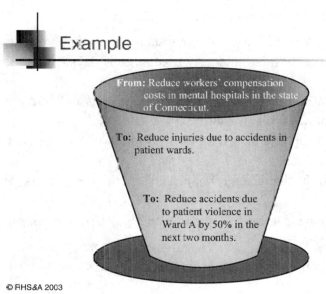

From: Reduce workers' compensation costs in mental hospitals in the state of Connecticut.

To: Reduce injuries due to accidents in patient wards.

To: Reduce accidents due to patient violence in Ward A by 50% in the next two months.

© RHS&A 2003

Figure 14-2. Breakthrough: Safety

Example

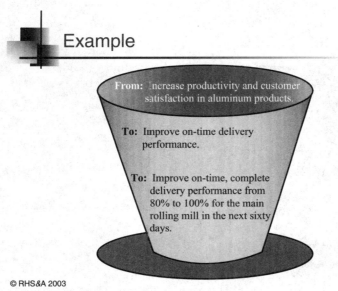

From: Increase productivity and customer satisfaction in aluminum products.

To: Improve on-time delivery performance.

To: Improve on-time, complete delivery performance from 80% to 100% for the main rolling mill in the next sixty days.

© RHS&A 2003

Figure 14-3. Breakthrough: Productivity

An execution breakthrough to create capability represents some basic improvements for the organization:

- Accomplishment of an end result, not just an activity that hopefully leads to a result. All the elements needed for the final payoff come together.
- A fundamental shift in direction or in the way things are done, not doing more of what you already are doing.
- Learning for everyone involved, not working harder or faster in well-worn routines.
- An opening for further change, not just an act once done that is the end.
- A clearly recognizable success against something that matters, not just a good try.

Here's an illustration of how it can work in practice:

Fred wanted to grow his plastic materials business, but he could not win new financing for expansions and new products. He had to get much more mileage out of his old facilities. He started by focusing on one set of extruders. He called on his managers and the extruder teams to see if they could get more quality production per day. Putting their heads together, they came up with a deliberate step-by-step plan and produced a 25-percent increase in one set of extruders in about six weeks.

The project required more than pushing more product through the machine on each production run. To achieve the goal, the plant had to reduce the changeover and cleanup time between runs, which meant a different changeover routine, and having cleaning supplies and spare parts immediately at hand. It had to get the warehouse to provide more raw materials every day, which in turn meant a faster order cycle from suppliers and more storage space near the extruding machines. It needed more frequent lab tests and faster lab response to assure on-spec quality at the higher output rate, and it needed better on-the-spot supervision to assure that bad product did not run on. It had to change the shipping routine to get more trucks onto the loading docks every morning to get product out the door. It required more frequent preventive maintenance inspections and lubrication to keep the machines working. Then, to get the benefit of the implied cost reduction, it meant closing down a lower-productivity unit, transferring some people, and letting a few others go.

Doing all this in a little more than a month was a whole new experience for the Production Department management team. They had to work directly with Warehouse, Shipping, Lab, Purchasing, Maintenance, and Human Resources people, as well as with their own staff, in a quite different way. Planning and carrying out this change was far different from following the normal work flow and complaining when parts were unavailable, or materials were short, or the lab was late getting test results back. They had to do a lot of joint planning. There were meetings almost every day to track the trial-and-error experiments to test new ideas. The sense of urgency was huge. Doing all this in just weeks required a pace of effort far beyond anything done before. Lots of old habits and psychological barriers fell by the wayside.

The lightning struck when, at the end, the whole system actually worked. People discovered they could get the same old machines and the same old people and the same old facilities to produce much more without new investment. You can imagine the elation of the management and manufacturing teams.

In twenty-first-century enterprises, execution must mean making productive changes such as these successfully as a matter of routine. Because changes like the ones described here are needed almost continuously, rapid execution has to be become a core capability. Adaptation must be feasible with far less stress and anguish than commonly occur in traditional operations. That happens as confidence and competence grow from repeated and successful practice of the disciplines of execution. Breakthrough projects are the vehicle for getting that practice.

The process of carving out a breakthrough project begins by defining a strategically crucial goal keyed to the readiness of people to do it. The people to be involved go through this exercise together. Hashing it out together, they think through the issues, expose their hidden assumptions, have them tested, consider alternatives, and argue out the best way to proceed. This kind of dialogue—sometimes hot and heavy—produces clarity and commitment. The leader's job is to push this process forward to get closure on the breakthrough goal.

While the big and strategically crucial goal might be scary, a small, success-laden increment makes it not only doable but exciting. It's easy to tell when people have defined something that will be a breakthrough—they share a moment of elation.

Define the Goal in Terms of End Results to Close Off Escape Routes

One of the most difficult challenges managers face is distinguishing between end-result goals and interim milestones, intermediate variables, or activities. It is important to do so because one of the chief reasons for execution shortfalls, especially in large and complex organizations, is failure to define and pursue the clear end-result goal. And this failure leads to proliferation of activity, work at cross purposes, and lack of coordination. It opens many escape routes when people encounter difficulties and frustrations. It is essential to work this through.

An end-result goal represents a visible, measurable, and tangible benefit to a customer, end user, shareholder, or other constituent: quality up, costs down, on-time delivery closer to 100 percent, profit up, response time faster, accidents down, more products launched in the marketplace successfully, and the like. These are different from goals such as analyses of cost reduction opportunities, systems installed, organization structures and staffing changed, people hired, products tested, financing raised. The latter are all preparatory or support steps. Such tasks are milestones in a result-focused project, but none of them *in themselves* actually generate bottom-line improvements for the company.

Small-Scale "Breakthrough Projects"

Interim Goals

One reason it is important to make this distinction is that while some preparatory or interim goals are essential to a project, such goals can be seductive, consuming endless streams of energy without ever producing a benefit for anyone. You've heard them: How can we reduce costs until we know more about where the money is being spent now? How can we improve production output if we don't have a baseline and an analysis of causes of delay? How can we improve our competitive position if we don't have benchmark data for each market segment? How can we expect better productivity if we don't have any data on output per person today? How can we reduce defects until we do accelerated life testing of various product configurations? How can we design better products if we don't research customer needs and desires first?

See, I told you these goals are seductive. The answer is you often can't. All of these can be essential steps on the path to achieving results. Work does have to be done on preparatory efforts. But preparatory projects are often used as smokescreens for underlying flaws behind many execution failures—such as failure to use what people already have or know or failure to achieve payoffs already available. The anxiety of confronting the end goal and facing up to demanding senior managers, persnickety customers, hungry shareholders, or other constituents can be so great that people find ways to put it off. And nothing is more comforting than activities that seem logical, sound good, feel good, are easy to do, and can conceivably make a contribution. Hiring consultants, buying big systems, and launching big training programs or vision and value and communication programs often fall into the category of classic and costly avoidance schemes.

Why gather more cost data when any management team can probably agree on two or three questionable costs that should undoubtedly be cut back? Why generate more reports and analyses when chances are the needed information is already buried somewhere in that yard-high pile of reports coming out of the computers each month? Why start another market study to understand your customers better when your top three customers (who happen to make up 20 percent of your business) have been pounding on the door for weeks about delayed delivery of new products or black specks in the pure white material you are delivering into their silos?

Problem Solving

Problem solving can be another smokescreen activity. People ask one another, How can we get new customers for insurance registered faster if we don't have complete application data? We have to solve the application data problem first. How can we reduce defects when we have faulty materials coming in from suppliers? We have to get better suppliers first. How can we expect better performance from workers without more competent supervisors? We have to solve the supervisor problem first. How can we improve if people aren't held accountable? We have to get the boss to hold people accountable first. And on and on. Or so it seems.

Solving a problem is not the same as achieving a result, unless it is built into an action plan to achieve the result. And results are rarely achieved by solving one problem or another. Complete insurance application data won't help much if you still have too few people at the registration desk to do the work. Getting better material from suppliers won't help if your incoming storage bins are dirty. Getting more supervisors might be important, but it won't help much if your supervisors are called into so many meetings that they aren't around enough to do any real supervising.

Shifting the Blame

A third way to hide involves attributing problems to other people or functions. "We can't manage our plants better with so many staff groups taking our people's time for their programs and meetings." "We've tried for years to get Distribution to sit down with us in Manufacturing to look at the cost of the whole delivery system. They claim the problem is our poor production planning."

Endless sequences of avoidance, blame, and partial efforts pop up when the end-result goal is not crystal clear and work is not carefully organized to produce the desired result. Like many of the other issues that interfere with successful execution, these factors can be minimized right up front by careful definition of the end result goal.

Design a Successful Breakthrough Project

A breakthrough project has five characteristics:

- *It has a specific, measurable end-result goal:* If the issue is, say, patient safety, a breakthrough goal would be "Injuries due to violence of patients reduced 50 percent in two months in Ward A." Not a study, not a new policy or procedure, not a new organization structure or training program with the hoped-for effect of reducing incidents, but an actual reduction in injuries compared to preceding periods.

- *It is achievable with the resources already available or easily secured:* Something the existing staff can do right now, without a major investment, a new crew of people, a new leader, a major reorganization, a new policy approved by the Board of Directors, or other time-consuming or diversionary preparatory activity.

- *It offers a bottom-line payoff:* When it is achieved, workers' compensation claims will be lower, quality production per dollar will be higher, and new profitable sales will increase. Activities such as meetings with ward nurses and staff, installation of larger orifices in extruding machines, or making more calls on new customers are not the same.

- *It involves and requires learning:* People will do things differently: use the disciplines of execution; discover ideas, motivation, and goodwill that weren't visible before; break out of comfortable but self-limiting routines. But it's focused learning—if the participants are just studying, preparing, gathering data, and visiting benchmarking sites, they aren't learning to execute.

- *Its success opens the way to further progress:* For example, the methods learned on one set of extruders can be applied to others; success in one ward can be replicated in other wards and other hospitals. If the results don't apply anywhere else, they're probably in the low-hanging-fruit class rather than a real breakthrough.

An effective goal statement states in very few words the specific end-result goal, how it is measured, and the date for achievement. Figure 14-4 illustrates the elements.

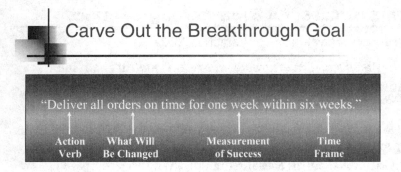

Carve Out the Breakthrough Goal

"Deliver all orders on time for one week within six weeks."

| Action Verb | What Will Be Changed | Measurement of Success | Time Frame |

© RHS&A 2003

Figure 14-4. Anatomy of a Breakthrough Goal

Use Small Successes to Build the Execution Culture

Cultural changes are, for the most part, achieved not through a master-stroke or massive reform effort but rather as the cumulative result of a series of many small advances. In contemporary management, this means projects that produce better performance, use better processes, and engage people more effectively. Projects of 30-, 60-, or 100-day duration begin to add up to the new culture. So in designing your effort, think through the projects that can be building blocks toward your strategic goal and also the kind of culture you want to have. Here's an example.

> A diversified manufacturer and distributor had to accelerate its product develop-ment cycle times to keep pace with worldwide competition. It started with just one product. A dedicated team with a special budget did in about one year some-thing that normally took three or four years, but it spent no more money than normal when it was all over.
>
> Then a Division of the Company, with a gun to its head to get its products out faster to meet market commitments, tackled three products to get the ball rolling on accelerated product cycles without a dedicated team or special budget but as part of normal operations. It narrowed the focus even more to accelerating one phase of the product cycle—moving from research into development.
>
> The experiment proved productive not only because the cycle time for this small part of the process was shortened but because a whole new way of manag-ing the product development job was invented and a new culture evolved. This

Small-Scale "Breakthrough Projects"

became standard operating procedure and ultimately was the basis for acceleration of the entire product program in the division, and then other divisions. The
new culture consisted of more parallel development steps versus serial steps,
more reuse of existing technologies rather than reinventing everything for every
new product, engaging downstream players up front, and focused accountability
on a prime project manager to drive accelerated development rather than letting
the old step-by-step process just play itself out. There was more collaboration
across functional lines as people in functional groups identified more closely with
the end product they were producing as well as their functional group.

A key part of the cultural shift was the move from a focus on prepa-
rations to a focus on results. Preparatory projects involved steps such as
solving a technical problem, arranging for adequate supplies, setting up
the factory to make the products along with the required test protocols
and equipment and staff, and field-testing, among many others. All these
were essential. But they were not the same as the project to produce the
end result. Instead, the prime product manager had to take total responsibility for getting the assigned product done and into the market successfully on the accelerated schedule while meeting quality, performance,
and budget specs. That was the end result; the responsible manager had
to pull together all the ingredients of effort needed to achieve the payoff.

Orchestrating all the elements to produce the end result is a fundamental pillar of execution. Small-scale breakthrough projects provide a
vehicle for inventing and learning what it takes to succeed in this complex task. Each small-scale success is a prototype and a building block for
integrating different strands of effort into an end result. The urgency of
the breakthrough project stimulates innovation, generating a higher
level of energy and enthusiasm. People have less time for excessive ana-
lyzing, studying, and preparing. For all these reasons, the breakthrough
project is the sparkplug for better, faster execution and a higher-perfor-
mance culture.

Breakthrough projects can be conceived at any stage of planning.
Candidates for breakthrough action can be identified as part of devising
and testing a strategy. Breakthrough projects can be created as part of a
launch meeting. They can be conceived as part of the detailed planning
of a project.

Execution, Plain and Simple

The reasons for the cultural impact of breakthrough projects are clear:

- They are genuine successes, not preparation for success.
- They provide very rapid feedback and reinforcement of the methodology used.
- Visible success proves to skeptics that it can be done.
- Participants learn how to overcome psychological and other organizational barriers.
- Success produces confidence, and with confidence, people are more willing to strike out for further gain.

15

Multiply Breakthrough Project Successes to Reach the Big Goals

Initial breakthrough successes create the essential foundation of experience with execution and high performance. The challenge, next, is to expand this experience and capability throughout the organization and achieve increasingly ambitious and far-reaching goals. Let's look at how this process unfolds—starting, again, with immediate opportunities.

Think for a moment. What are the most important and urgent bottom-line end results to be produced? Lower costs? Higher quality? More revenue? More profit?

Next, what are the most important and urgent cultural changes to be made, changes in the way the organization functions? This means changes such as more focus on overall goals versus subgroup goals, more collaboration versus competition among units, stepping up the level of responsibility that people take, getting things done on time, more effective relationships with customers, simplification of procedures, internal communications, and the like.

It is important to make two lists: the end results first, and the cultural or organizational shifts second.

Sometimes managers will start working on the cultural shifts on the assumption that results will follow. But that can be a fallacy. It is important to be clear about the actual end results to be sought before considering changes in behavior and ways of working.

Pick one goal and group to start. One manager did it in an afternoon, like this:

> Al, head of fossil-fueled production for an urban electric utility company, attended a breakfast seminar on execution and was struck by the idea of setting better demands. That afternoon, he called in his manager of maintenance and insisted that the next planned outage (shutdown of a piece of equipment for maintenance and repair) had to come in on schedule and on budget. He would no longer accept cost overruns and delayed completion on predictable major repairs. The two agreed on the next project to focus on. Two months later, the project did come in on time and on budget—a first in years. "The only change I made was to ask much more clearly—in fact insist on it—for on-schedule and on-budget performance. The demand just had not been clear before," Al said.

The point is that you don't have to construct a large-scale and complex program to start to upgrade execution. Pick something to work on. Tackle that objective with the dual aim of producing a success and learning from the experience. Then build on the success to move step by step to more far-reaching and broader advances. But get a feel for the whole process of improving execution and the disciplines outlined in this book in a few limited and focused areas first. That foundation of experience is vital.

Tap the Hidden Reserve

When you are ready to enlist your group and move to broader objectives, you can call a meeting for the purpose. The main focus should be the goal you want to tackle.

In the meeting you can start with the exercise of estimating the potential for gain by tapping hidden reserves (introduced in Chapter 13). Once you have an estimate of how much you might gain, then get back to your specific goal. Carve out specific, short-term incremental results. Appoint people to lead the efforts to achieve the goals. Define solid assignments (this will take some thorough discussion). Set dates for the first progress reviews and offer to provide whatever help makes sense. It can be that simple.

Jim carved out a full day with his management team in his company's newly purchased business. Jim's assignment was to supercharge earnings and growth. "How about 25 percent per year profit and revenue growth?" asked the company's president. Jim knew it wasn't a question, it was a charge, and he would be judged against that standard. Jim shared that charge with his team.

They had a lot of issues to deal with. Most of the top executives of the prior company were gone. Quickly, Jim's new team had to learn to manage the business better and find competent people in the ranks. To get that kind of growth, the company would have to get into the consumer market, quite different from its traditional commercial customer base. It would have to gear up for new digital technology. Prices were coming down, but the business was saddled with high overheads. So costs had to come down too. Another issue was delivery. In Jim's first round of meetings with key customers, they all said, "Get it to us when you promise it."

All these issues and more bounced around the room for several hours. Jim insisted that the group pick a starting point for change that day. "This new team has to create some solid successes to get the organization moving," he said.

Tony, head of product development, marketing, and sales, proposed a new product launch as a focal point. Getting a success here would be an eye-opener for the organization and a shot in the arm for the income statement. It would also be a good test of whether, as Jim had suggested, there really was hidden potential in the organization. (Tony, having been in the organization for several years, was skeptical about that.) The group agreed and thought through the assignment to Tony and a lead engineer.

Jim then turned to his manager of manufacturing and asked him to start a project on delivery improvement. That assignment too was thought through with the group.

In this example, two projects were defined and started in one day. Both proved successful in subsequent weeks. A series of other projects followed, driving up delivery performance, productivity, new product introductions, and earnings substantially—in the first quarter.

There are three main areas of opportunity for expansion of breakthrough action throughout an organization: operations, strategy, and infrastructure.

Creating Operations Breakthroughs

Operations breakthroughs improve production output, productivity, quality, sales, delivery, customer satisfaction, collections—the key variables of day-to-day performance. Projects aiming at operations breakthroughs have multiple payoffs. They get more and better work done with less time and energy. They improve efficiency by reducing the drain of energy and goodwill caused by error, rework, returned goods, and customer inquiries and complaints, all voracious consumers of time and energy.

These breakthroughs help improve control by shifting the tone of the organization from crisis management and tactical problem solving to more orderly and persistent pursuit of improved performance. Operational gains raise morale and customer satisfaction. They build the credibility of the organization as a reliable producer. They are also the vehicle for building execution capability in the front ranks—with the people who make and deliver products and services, the people who are in day-to-day contact with customers, the people who make or break the company's reputation.

Operational improvement is a relatively highly refined aspect of management practice in U.S. companies and leading companies worldwide. Industrial engineering, quality management, process reengineering, automation, digitization, and Six Sigma processes are some of the well-developed and well-practiced methods to support operational improvement. The opportunity for operational improvement is limitless, not only within an organization but across supply chains and value chains of all kinds. You can always do more to improve performance and to build execution capability at the operational level. Here are a few examples:

Chase Bank worked on ATM performance to reduce outages and maintenance costs.

In Morgan Bank, 14 operations departments reduced costs and improved turnaround time on transactions.

State mental hospitals in Connecticut reduced accidents and injuries and workman's compensation claims.

Other hospitals have reduced waiting time in X-ray units, patient care errors, and losses of equipment and tools such as dressing sets and IV poles.

Multiply Breakthrough Project Successes

A Federal Reserve Bank reduced security costs, paper and supply costs, check processing operations costs, and delays.

Pharmaceutical companies have speeded new drug application cycle times and increased productivity of research labs.

In all these cases, and many more, the gains were achieved just through better execution. Managers provided clear, tough assignments. Teams developed and tested their strategies. They had kickoff events and built solid work plans. They followed up hard, communicated along the way, and closed out with successes. The people involved in the work units created on-the-job innovations that made better use of resources already available.

More sophisticated operations improvement efforts such as Six Sigma and process reengineering and systems development efforts require more investment. They can be big winners, to the extent that they are carried out primarily by the initiative and energy of the people in the organization. Some are not, however. When they are consultant- or staff-driven efforts, they require big investments up front with the promise of results to come in the future. Too many of these kinds of projects have turned into traps—generating cost, putting off benefits, and precluding growth of the people in the organization. Be wary of these kinds of externally driven, preparations-first operations improvement programs.

Creating Strategic Breakthroughs

Strategic breakthroughs create new products, new services, new alliances, new business models, and fundamentally different operating platforms for a competitive edge. The literature on strategic planning is vast. Consultants by the hordes do research and propose new strategies for virtually any purpose—and they can be good strategies.

The crucial issue is implementing a new strategy successfully. This is far from a trivial matter. The annals of business history are full of strategic failures, as are the pages of the *Wall Street Journal* and the *Financial Times* and the *New York Times* and *Business Week,* to mention just a few purveyors of management embarrassment. Companies need to develop capability for strategic change. And this means capability to carry out strategic change successfully, not just do research, draft strategic plans, and launch good tries.

The great and enduring companies seem to have this capacity. Think about the evolution of General Electric over the twentieth century. Or IBM. Or Johnson & Johnson. Or 3M. Under the surface, you find that their great transformations actually have not been such heroic overnight transformations as they might seem. Instead, these companies maintain constant experimentation and testing of new ideas, new people, and new ways of doing things. In other words, they use a continuing stream of modest strategic breakthroughs to show the way and build the competence and momentum which adds up to major changes.

Strategic breakthroughs are keyed to a new direction you want to pursue. For example:

GE Capital focused on acquisitions as a strategic direction. Acquisitions, like marriages, don't have a particularly wonderful success rate. They are strategic changes because they create new arms of an enterprise, bringing together different cultures that have to be integrated in ways far from simply operating from day to day. GE Capital generated considerably higher success rates in this arena by codifying and applying highly disciplined methods that were applied and refined over and over again, beginning with focused attention to just a few immediate acquisition deals (Ashkenas, 1998).

Avery-Dennison launched an accelerated growth effort for its worldwide business, making labels and related applications of print and adhesives. To generate more bottom-line payoff from growth, the company stimulated a series of short-term breakthrough growth projects to exploit opportunities near at hand— what they called Level I growth, to augment the longer-term research and development efforts, which they called Level II and III growth. They started with one business unit and five teams. Expanding on these first successes, they moved division by division, ultimately throughout the entire company. People on the front lines, working with their customers, invented and launched more than 200 small-scale, rapid-cycle growth projects over a period of a year and a half. These produced revenue growth of $150 million in the face of a very tough market and built widespread strategic execution capability at the same time.

After a series of operational breakthroughs, the Plastics Company managers (Chapter 14) launched a series of conferences to map out a huge array of new applications and a huge batch of new properties for its materials to meet the needs of these applications. This was the starting point for sustained growth in the breadth of the business. Step-by-step, strategic breakthrough projects were then used to build new materials for autos and for industrial and consumer needs. These fueled tripling of the business over a period of three years, again in the face of some very tough economic times.

These kinds of strategic execution capabilities are at the heart of what Gary Hamel and Liisa Valikangas (2003) have called the "quest for resilience." With the growing turbulence of business worldwide, they pointed out the need for organizational capacity for constant strategic change.

Infrastructure Change

When asked how they think they can best improve their business, many managers answer with infrastructure changes. "We'll install a new information system." "We'll step up our training and upgrade hiring standards." "We'll reorganize and go to strategic business units instead of functional structure." "We'll come up with a strategic plan to enter new markets." "We'll reengineer our processes." Fantasyland!

If you want to improve your business, you have to focus on end results—sell more products at better margins to more customers. If you want to hold on to your customers and cut attrition, you have to deliver better call center service and better products cheaper. If you want a competitive edge, you need a better product or service that actually provides more value to customers. The displacement of focus to infrastructure from end results is a common delusion of management practice.

In the context of disciplined pursuit of bottom-line goals, however, infrastructure change can provide enormous leverage if the infrastructure change is in synchronization with operations improvement and strategic changes. Infrastructure changes can help a great deal and even stimulate bottom-line change, but they can't substitute for it.

The 12 steps of execution apply very well to execution of infrastructure projects. There is little that is more exciting than to have information systems installations come up on time, on budget, and really working when you are counting on them to help create new kinds of customer services or to streamline processes and reduce costs. Infrastructure improvement applies also to modernizing outmoded human resources systems and practices, streamlining supply chains, and upgrading customer service responsiveness.

PNC Financial's IT people dramatically reduced cost and speeded the installation of the company's first corporatewide retail sales system by breaking it down into a series of very focused breakthrough projects. Each installation team set a sharp goal, strategy, work plan, and follow-up process to bring its piece of the installation in on time and budget. At the same time, the member banks were required to carry out sales and productivity improvement projects in synch with the system installation. Those plans were their admission tickets to participation in the information system. The chairman issued the charge to improve branch sales and productivity. The head of Systems and Operations set the challenge to the IT people. The systems development teams responded using disciplined execution processes. The installation costs came down 26 percent, the overall installation cycle was cut almost in half, and branch sales performance and productivity grew. The same approach was then replicated in other major systems and became standard procedure.

Be a Demanding Developmental Leader

None of the good things of execution happen by themselves. They happen because leaders demand that they happen, in ways that are effective. And they support the development of capability of their people. As Steve Kerr said when he was head of GE's Crotonville management development center, "It is immoral to demand extraordinary performance without providing help so that people can succeed." That's why Jack Welch spent so much time and energy at the Center. That is why Kerr and a large corps of experts worked throughout the company, as well as in GE's Crotonville Center, to stimulate, teach, and support growth of capability under the banner of various GE strategic drives.

Zeke B. demonstrated the lessons very well. He ran a plant making cooking oils, toothpaste, and detergents. The company was looking to Zeke to upgrade the whole operation. It was old. The equipment was worn. Long-term employees were a discouraged lot. The main driveway entering the plant was cracked and settling. Performance was poor. Zeke called for help. The plant needed new managers, new people, new equipment, and lots of capital. None of it was forthcoming. "I need all these things and they send me a consultant," Zeke fumed.

Headquarters refused to send in more resources because they didn't think they would be used well. The organization was in a constant fire-fighting mode—patching one thing here, running around a problem there. All energy was consumed just struggling to keep up with day-to-day shipments and fend off disasters.

Multiply Breakthrough Project Successes

The consultants proposed to work with Zeke to apply all the things in this book. It worked. A turnaround was achieved, and the key lesson was the subtle but nevertheless powerful shift in the way Zeke managed.

Instead of running after problems day after day himself in an attempt to help his people cope, he slowly but clearly turned the tables. He began asking his people, in one focused area at a time, to take charge of some improvement and make it happen.

The consultants could help organize the improvement work, but it was the managers' responsibility. In Maintenance, emergency work orders were cut back by a concentrated repair drive. The Packaging Department's machine output crept upward, and waste from leaking and dropped product declined as supervisors and workers took responsibility for making these things happen. Each of these projects had its leader, core team, goals and measurements, work plans, kickoff events, follow-up processes and communications, and each closed on its results with dispatch.

As the organization began to function better, headquarters people began to change their posture as well. In one case, Zeke knew that 10 new detergent dryers would have great payoff. But headquarters refused to approve the purchase. When he changed his stance and asked for just one, they approved. When it became clear to headquarters that the dryer really did pay off, they supported purchase of the next nine.

Step by step, other investments helped as well. But the main drive was execution first led by Zeke and the people who stood up and took charge of projects he and they created. His ability to create demands and provide help fundamentally changed the behavior pattern of the organization and the results achieved. Once again, the hidden reserve came into play as the same busy people, with the same equipment, and the same facilities produced more just because they set higher expectations and executed better to meet them.

These principles apply to an organization of any size. A work group supervisor, a department head, a strategic business unit leader, a division, sector, or corporate leader can apply these principles to their own groups. Only the size and scope of the undertaking differs.

While it is possible to generate widespread and pervasive execution progress across an organization, and build superlative performance thereby, remember, it all can start with a single goal. It can start today. The key is to get started—and then follow through with the 12 steps on each project.

16

The Senior Management Task: Focus Your Organization on the Few Most Crucial Goals

To this point, this book has focused first on steps to execute on an assignment or an opportunity, then on ways to accelerate the progress of a company on a broader and broader scale. But what about setting those overriding strategic goals in the first place? This chapter outlines ways to carry out the senior management task of setting the compelling strategic goals that drive big gains and excellent execution. Such focus is key.

As a senior manager, you have many choices about what to do. But one thing you *must* do. Choose. Get your organization focused on, committed to, and acting on a few truly crucial big goals.

Organizations often have too many goals. They swim in a sea of objectives, initiatives, priority projects, and other pseudonyms for the bewildering activity that substitutes for the hard work of thinking things through, defining what is really important, and executing.

It is easy to rationalize this proliferation of activity, especially in large and complex organizations. Senior managers often see their role as creating general directions and letting people down the line set their own goals as they see fit within that strategic framework. It is hard to argue with this logic. But if external conditions have changed radically, if the results are not what they should be, if commitments are not being met, or if people are deferring, recasting numbers, or crossing their fingers in the hope that, in time, the results will be there, a different tactic is needed.

Proliferation of activity is also a common escape mechanism for managers overwhelmed by change, unsure about their direction, or queasy about their ability to achieve their goals. "Look at all the things we're doing" sounds good, even though it might really mean they are pursuing endless activity while crucial end results don't change for the better.

To drive significantly better performance and excellent execution, select the few most crucial goals. That is, select the few goals that are tough enough, important enough, and urgent enough to drive action from top to bottom. These crucial goals provide focus that concentrates energy on important things and squeezes out off-target and low-payoff activity. Most important, with only a few goals, people have no place to hide. The goals are right in front of everyone. Just as in a crisis, unwavering concentration on the overriding goal produces huge surges in performance.

You might well be thinking, "Sure, we would execute better if we did only one or two things. We've done it many times. But now we must keep a lot of things going because. . . ." Or, "the boss won't take anything off the table. He insists that we do it all."

Nearly every time my colleagues and I worked with an organization that agreed to make a concerted drive toward a few crucial goals, nothing else suffered in the process of reaching those goals. The productivity of the whole organization seemed to grow under the impetus of the breakthrough efforts and the change in climate that occurs during such drives. It turned out to be possible to both achieve the crucial goals and cover virtually everything else. In some cases, people found plenty of off-strategy activity that could be (and was) stopped. In most cases, however, the initial concern about losing ground was a reflection of anxiety associated with tackling the crucial goals. Once successes were being achieved, anxiety declined. Almost unconsciously the organization accomplished more because the whole climate of execution had taken a big step up—a kind of bonus payoff beyond the payoff from achieving the crucial goals.

Getting Focused

Sometimes the focal points are imposed from the outside. The need to respond to a major competitive threat can be one driving force. The demands of shareholders to take the earnings or growth rate up might be another. Serious unhappiness of a major customer can be another. The once-in-a-lifetime chance to get into a new market, pick up a major customer, or acquire a new technology or partner might be another. The crucial goals in such cases are self-evident. The point is that these can also be the focus of conscious effort to upgrade execution discipline at the same time. Applying and practicing the 12 steps for execution in pursuit of such goals will help accelerate achievement and reinforce the basic disciplines and habits of execution.

If proliferation is an issue, and external forces are not setting clear and unavoidable demands, then you set such goals yourself with your management team. Call a meeting of your key people for the specific purpose of sorting through the work programs underway and to contemplate ways to narrow down to the goals that *must* be achieved. At the meeting, propose some definitions for setting the crucial few goals. For example:

- *Survival:* Things to be done to assure sustained success of the business and avoid falling back. You can usually find plenty to do right here to upgrade customer service, sales, productivity, quality, costs, collections, and otherwise improve vital factors of customer satisfaction and earnings. The risk in doing these things is low; the risk in not doing them is high. These can be operational breakthrough projects.

- *Competitive Edge:* These are more far-reaching advances in products and services, market strategy, delivery, technology, and streamlining of processes. These are steps to significantly differentiate you

Hierarchy of Goals

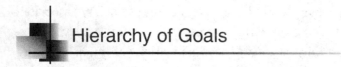

Climb the Ladder of Success

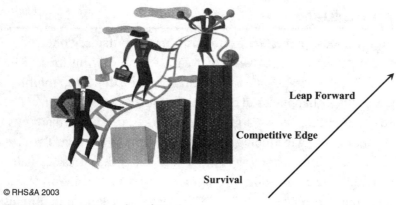

Leap Forward

Competitive Edge

Survival

© RHS&A 2003

Figure 16-1. Hierarchy of Goals

from competitors and provide or extend a competitive edge. These can be operational and strategic breakthroughs.

- *Leap Forward:* Higher-risk ventures such as acquisitions, major research and development efforts, or significant shifts in the nature of the business or the organization. Actions in this class create a whole new thrust for the business if not for the industry. These can be strategic breakthroughs.

Clearly, if you have survival matters on the table, this may not be the time to be working toward a high risk leap forward. The three categories form a hierarchy to help prioritize commitments, as illustrated in Figure 16-1.

Ask yourself, Where are we in this hierarchy? What is crucial for us? A hierarchy such as this helps keep people focused on the things that count so they don't spend energy on higher-level ventures to the detriment of the basic business. Higher-level and leap-forward ventures can make sense when the organization has tremendous momentum on the lower levels.

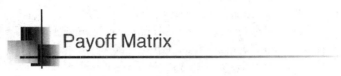

Payoff Matrix

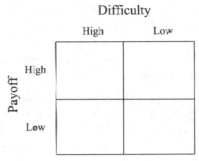

© RHS&A 2003

Figure 16-2. Payoff Matrix

After listing items in these categories, you can sort them further with a common matrix to differentiate the high-payoff/easy goals from those with lower payoff or more difficulty (Figure 16-2). Classify each goal and put it in the appropriate quadrant. Those that go in the upper right, the high-payoff/easy goals, warrant first consideration as the crucial choices.

These are basic tools that can serve well without a great deal of analytical work. People often know enough about the relative payoff of and effort required for various projects. They can make reasonable judgments and are all too willing to sort through the maze and define truly vital efforts.

It is important to do this sorting with your management team. You might have some conflict, as different camps line up behind different goals. Good. The debate will sharpen the case for going after them. You can push for unanimous consent, count votes to get to the final selection, or make your own decision. In any case you'll see where the energy is, who is ready to take the ball and run. You'll have your crucial few goals and your constituency to go for them.

The outcome of this exercise might be a list of three to six major objectives. There is no magic number for the right array of imperatives. But *focus* is vital. Here's a case to illustrate this approach:

187

Execution, Plain and Simple

Jerry, general manager of a specialty manufacturing business, focused his organization to turn around the performance and strategic direction of the business. The organization was flooded with urgent improvement projects, modernizations, retraining programs, and the like, but results were just not coming out the other end, and serious losses persisted. Jerry called a series of working conferences of his leadership team. First, he proposed just one goal—getting the business to break even. His people nodded, though not enthusiastically. "What's new?" they thought. Then he asked the group to select a date by which breakeven would be achieved. The votes came back ranging from six months to three years. Clearly there was no agreement on a date, and this meant there was no agreed-upon strategy for getting to break even despite the enormous number of projects underway purporting to improve profitability.

Jerry called another conference, for two days off-site, to select the projects most likely to get the business to break even by year-end (nine months away). He told the group that he meant break even for the full year, not just a breakeven run rate by year end, a much harder goal. People were asked to prepare for the conference by generating their own list of proposals, and also to define what the division had to do differently to succeed.

At the conference, the group at first balked at the goal. But Jerry held his ground, insisting that people focus on achieving it. He and the group worked through the list of nominated projects and narrowed them down to three that seemed most doable and most likely to produce a big increment toward the breakeven goal. One project was to reduce front-end order processing cost and speed up order handling with an automated information system. A second project was to boost sales of a new product to the Japanese market. A third project called for getting one new product up and running on an automated high-speed/low-cost production line, rather than automate the whole factory. He asked that each project be carried out in no more than three months. And he assigned a leader and people to lead each. Small subteams were commissioned to draft the formal assignment and specs for the projects in a week.

Jerry also pulled together a summary of views—the group's and his own—on the changes needed in the culture of the organization. They would shift from being primarily a strategic supplier to a profitable supplier. They would shift from focusing mainly on their technology to focusing mainly on their customers and meeting customer needs. They would shift from accepting studies, recommendations, and good tries and insist on getting targeted results.

Sharp and intense focus on the three initial payoff projects was a radical departure from the past pattern of work. The projects were called "prime" projects. They were not easy picking. Each was a "reach out" project. Jerry set up meetings to review the formal assignments, and he asked the project leaders to prepare work plans in two weeks. Then, in two weeks, he set up review sessions with the project leaders and their core teams to review the work plans for the projects. Some were rejected and had to be redone several times until they were clearly targeted or the goal and were complete enough to be successful. Then he got out to the whole organization, department by department, to describe what the management team was doing and to call on every part of the division to support the "prime" projects as their first priority. He also reviewed each department's work program and began cutting back on nonstrategic activity, anything keyed to its past role as a unique, protected strategic operation rather than a profit maker. Tough progress reviews were held with the prime project teams one at a time at least every two weeks to review what had been done and to plot out specific next steps to overcome problems and push forward.

Three months later, in the next off-site conference, Jerry and the management team reconvened. Substantial, in fact surprising, progress had been made. The group selected three additional projects from their original list. People were much less reluctant to take leadership responsibility this time. They saw that success was happening. People were fighting for prime project leadership and other assignments on the new projects. Continuing this process, the team pushed through the full breakeven target by year-end and kept the profit curve climbing year after year. Focus on prime projects became the normal mode of management, no longer reserved just for special efforts.

There are no real shortcuts in this process of setting crucial goals. Yes, benchmarking studies can help you find where you stand versus competitors. You can have consulting studies done. You can write memos commanding attention to the crucial goals as you see them. These tend to be low-yield tactics. In the last analysis, there is no substitute for getting your people engaged with you in thinking through to the crucial goals and committing to executing. There is no alternative but to do this hard work.

To document the results of this work with your leadership team, write down the crucial goals. Also, in a few short phrases or sentences, list what is to change: the key shifts you need to make from what, to what, to achieve the goals and work more effectively. Figures 16-3 and 16-4 illustrate ways of portraying the crucial goals. At the end of this chapter, you'll find a worksheet to assist in the process. To build understanding and commitment throughout the organization beyond your leadership team, you can present and discuss this document over and over again

Strategically Crucial Goals

Mission

Design, manufacture, and distribute best-in-class electronic communication products for industrial use worldwide.

Strategically Crucial Goals

To overcome competition from Japan:

■ Win new contract for sale of products in Japan to demonstrate our ability to compete

■ Speed new product development cycles by 50%

■ Reduce product costs 10% per year for the next three years

© RHS&A 2003

Figure 16-3. Strategically Crucial Goals

with managers at all levels. As the managers become convinced of the rightness of the goals, they will be able to articulate the same goals themselves and stimulate their people to act on them.

Looking Ahead

You now have the whole picture of execution plain and simple:

- Twelve steps to execute on any goal
- One strategy for using short-term, rapid-cycle breakthrough projects to accelerate progress and build execution capability throughout an organization
- A top management job to define and lead pursuit of the few most crucial goals that lift the organization to exemplary performance

With the crucial few goals firmly in hand, you can go back to the beginning of the book and have your people use the 12 steps to execute successfully on these crucial goals. With success, you can move to a second cycle of goals, and so on. Step by step, quarter by quarter, year by year, you can lead your organization to perform better, faster, and with greater ease and efficiency. And that is what we mean by execution, plain and simple.

Strategically Crucial Goals—
Key Shifts

From What	To What
■ Serial product development process	■ Parallel product development process
■ Dispersed accountability	■ Pinpointed "prime" accountability
■ Functional structures dominant	■ Project structures dominant
■ Highly complex approval process	■ Simple, rapid-cycle approval process
■ Many parts and options	■ Few basic product platforms
■ Reinvent everything for every product	■ Adapt what we have

© RHS&A 2003

Figure 16-4. Strategically Crucial Goals: Key Shifts

WORKSHEET:

Crucial Goals

What is the gap between where your organization is and where it must be with respect to performance and competitive position? What goals must be met?

_____

_____

_____

_____

_____

_____

_____

_____

WORKSHEET: (*Continued*)

What changes in organization and culture are needed for success?

From What	To What

What next steps will you take to mobilize action on your crucial goals? _____

_____

_____

_____

References

Ashkenas, R. N., Frances, S. C., and DeMonaco, L. J. "Make the Deal Real: How GE Integrates Acquisitions." *Harvard Business Review* (January-February 1998): 165–178.

Bossidy, L., and Charan, R. *Execution: The Discipline of Getting Things Done* (New York: Crown Business, 2002).

Collins, J. *Good to Great* (New York: HarperBusiness, 2001).

Hamel, G., and Valikangas, L. "The Quest for Resilience." *Harvard Business Review* (September 2003): 52–65.

Matta, N., and Ashkenas, R. "Why Good Projects Fail Anyway." *Harvard Business Review* (September 2003): 109–116.

Nohria, N., Robertson, B., and Joyce, B. "What Really Works." *Harvard Business Review* (July 2003): 42–55.

Schaffer, R. H. *The Breakthrough Strategy: Using Short-Term Successes to Build the High Performance Organization* (New York: HarperBusiness, 1988).

Ulrich, D., Kerr, S., and Ashkenas, R. *The GE Work-Out: How to Implement GE's Revolutionary Method for Busting Bureaucracy and Attacking Organizational Problems—Fast!* (New York: McGraw-Hill, 2002).

Index

Note: **Boldface** numbers indicate illustrations or tables.

Index

Index

Index

Index

About the Author

Robert A. Neiman holds an M.B.A. from Harvard and is a partner in the management consulting firm of Robert H. Schaffer & Associates. He and his associates have consulted for such companies as Allied Signal, CNA Financial, General Electric, Motorola, PNC Financial, and many others. He has published numerous articles on execution.

Robert H. Schaffer & Associates has pioneered the theory and practice of managing change and building high-performing organizations for over forty years. Based in Stamford, Connecticut, the firm helps organizations achieve rapid improvements in results, sustain progress, and link strategic planning, organization development and operational innovation to succeed in rapidly changing environments.